TWO UNCOMFORTABLE HISTORICAL TRUTHS

Black History Before Slavery Biblical History is Black History

KENNETH BROWN

Copyright © 2025

"Two Uncomfortable Historical Truths: Black History Before Slavery | Biblical History is Black History"
By Kenneth Brown

No part of this book may be reproduced, stored in or introduced into a retrieval system, or transmitted, in any form or by any means (electronic, mechanical, photocopying, recording, or otherwise) without prior written permission from the publisher.

ISBN: 979-8-9989246-0-6

The scriptures in this book were taken from the King James Version (KJV) – Bible in Public Domain; New International Version (NIV), Holy Bible, New International Version, NIV Copyright 1973, 1978, 1984, 2011 by Biblica, English Standard Version (ESV), New Revised Standard Version, Christian Standard Bible, New King James Version (NKJV), Amplified Bible, Revised Standard Version, The Message, Contemporary English Version, American Standard Version, Tyndale Bible, Good News Bible, New American Bible, The Living Bible, etc. All rights reserved worldwide.

For information on the content of this book,
email: xrayken3@yahoo.com

JMPinckney Publishing, LLC
JMPinckneyPublishing@gmail.com

Printed in the United States of America

Dedication

I must tell my story because it is different
from the story told about me.
To my daughter Patrice Nicole Richardson
who insisted that I not let the revelations
of my research accompany me to the grave.

Contents

Dedication iii
Foreword vii
Introduction ix

Part One: Ancient Africans in Early America 1

Chapter One: African Presence in Prehistoric America 2
Chapter Two: Pre-Columbian Presence of Africans in Early America 4
Chapter Three: The Grand Canyon 12
Chapter Four: The Mystery City of Cahokia 16
Chapter Five: Ancient Africans South of The Border 25

Part Two: Ancient Africans Around The World 33

Chapter Six: Ancient Egypt's 3,000 Years of World Dominance 34
Chapter Seven: Ancient Africans in Early China 43
Chapter Eight: Chinese Scientist Awakens to A Foundational Truth 53
Chapter Nine: A Tale of Two Rich African Brothers 57
Chapter Ten: Out of Africa Came Eve 69
Chapter Eleven: The Mother of us all, Mitochondria Eve 72

Part Three: The Bible is the Black Man's History 111

Chapter Twelve: The Bible is the Black Man's History #1 112
Chapter Thirteen: The Bible is the Black Man's History #2 122
Chapter Fourteen: The Bible is the Black Man's History #3 132

Part Four: An Uncomfortable Truth about Jesus of Nazareth 141

Chapter Fifteen: An uncomfortable Truth about Jesus of Nazareth #1 142
Chapter Sixteen: An uncomfortable truth about Jesus of Nazareth #2 152
Chapter Seventeen: An uncomfortable truth about Jesus of Nazareth #3 161
References 168

FOREWORD

Why do you think that most African Americans are unaware of our history pre-slavery? Let's explore some reasons.

One lesser-known reason why there is so little written information to counter the Western fallacy of white supremacy is the fact that Europeans carefully preserved their history through well-stocked and well-maintained libraries while simultaneously and systematically destroying hundreds of thousands of ancient manuscripts. This explains, in part, why there are so few written accounts of ancient Black historical events and achievements.

Thousands of books from pre-Columbian America (yes, there were books in the Americas prior to the arrival of Columbus.) were destroyed. Bishop Diego de Landa Calderón of Spain oversaw this campaign, saying, "burn them all, they are the work of the Devil."

Close to a million books were destroyed when Europeans ransacked the culturally advanced Egyptian city of Alexandria. This city's magnificent libraries were burned to the ground—but not before Greek scholars made off with hundreds of books on science, mathematics, engineering, philosophy, and more.

Thousands of books were burned when the culturally sophisticated city of Timbuktu was leveled on two occasions.

In response to orders by Cardinal Jimenez, Europeans destroyed eighty-four thousand books written by the Black Moors. The Moors dominated Europe during the Dark Ages and established an oasis of governmental, educational, and cultural sophistication. They were finally driven out in 1942.

Another reason (and this is an indictment) why we are not familiar with our pre-slavery history is that we do not have faith in the works of our Black scholars. We do not read their books nor attend their lectures. Some of these scholars—like Ivan Van Sertima, Cheikh Anta Diop, John Henry Clarke, and Dr. Yosef Ben Jochannan—have toiled for decades documenting our history, but we have been brainwashed into being suspicious of historical facts not presented by white historians. Other ethnic groups hold their historians in the highest esteem and rely on them to accurately tell their stories. Sadly, we have come to the point where we pay little or no attention to the work of our black scholars and appear insensitive to their tireless efforts to educate us.

Yet another reason is that we do not control any of the sources we depend on for information. We don't control what's aired on television or the radio; we don't control what is printed in the media; we don't control the movies produced; and we certainly don't control the content taught in our educational institutions.

INTRODUCTION

UNVEILING THE HIDDEN PAST

For centuries, the narrative surrounding Black history began with the horrors of the transatlantic slave trade. This book shatters that limited perspective, embarking on a groundbreaking journey to explore the rich and vibrant tapestry of Black history before the arrival of Europeans.

We begin by delving into the truth surrounding the founding of the Americas. Did Christopher Columbus truly discover a "New World"? Or were there earlier visitors who left their mark on the continent? We'll explore the pre-Columbian African presence in North America, from the survival of the holocaust of Slavery by The Black Washitaw Nation, to the routing of British settlers during the Yamasee war.

This is a story of empires, innovation, and forgotten contributions. We'll explore the Egyptian sojourn in the Grand Canyon, the enigmatic city of Cahokia, and the ongoing debate surrounding the ancient Washitaw Nation. We'll confront the concept of a "stolen legacy" where the achievements of Africans have been attributed to other cultures.

Shifting our focus southward, we'll explore the legacies of powerful African civilizations, such as the Olmecs, and their connection to

Africa, challenging traditional narratives about their origins. The controversial figure of Thor Heyerdahl sought to prove that ancient Africans possessed the capability for transatlantic travel. We'll also explore the possibility of ancient African ships capable of undertaking such voyages and celebrate Black Mariners navigational know-hows.

Prepare to be surprised as we explore the African presence in prehistoric America, long before Columbus stumbled into the Caribbean.

This book ventures beyond the Americas, uncovering the fascinating connections between ancient African and Chinese cultures. We'll travel to early China, where evidence suggests a dominant African presence in China's Xia and Shang dynasties.

Focusing on the powerful Ancient African Empires that existed long before the Europeans invaded, we look at the Egyptian Empire and the West African Empire of Mali. We highlight the leadership of two remarkable brothers, Abubakari and Mansa Musa, whose reigns in Mali brought immense wealth and prestige to the empire. Mansa Musa, the wealthiest ruler in history, transformed Mali into an empire of unparalleled wealth and prosperity.

Finally, we return to the very origins of humanity, exploring the fascinating theory of "Out of Africa," which posits that modern humans originated on the continent. We'll also delve into the concept of Mitochondrial Eve, the matriarchal ancestor of all modern humans. And delve into the scientific evidence that rewrites our understanding of human origins, placing Mitochondrial Eve firmly in Africa.

THE BIBLE IS BLACK HISTORY

Throughout history, the Bible has been a sacred text that has shaped the faith, culture, and identity of millions. Yet, within its pages lies a narrative that has often been overlooked, rewritten, or dismissed—the undeniable presence of Black history. This book aims to illuminate those hidden truths, shedding light on the people, places, and events that connect the Bible to Africa's rich and diverse heritage and its descendants.

From the earliest accounts of powerful and influential women to the often-misrepresented image of Jesus of Nazareth, the Bible is filled with figures who were deeply intertwined with the African continent and its people. The dominant Eurocentric interpretations of biblical figures have shaped how we perceive them today, often stripping them of their true cultural and ethnic identities. However, a closer examination of the scriptures, historical records, and archaeological discoveries reveals a different reality—one that celebrates the Black presence in biblical history.

WOMEN IN THE BIBLE: THE UNSEEN MATRIARCHS

The influence of Black women in the Bible is profound, yet their stories have frequently been overshadowed. These women were leaders, warriors, and pivotal figures in shaping the course of biblical history. From the wisdom of the Queen of Sheba to the courage of Queen Esther, their lives challenge the traditional narratives that have ignored their significance. By reclaiming their stories, we not only honor their contributions but also recognize the impact of Black women in shaping faith and society.

JESUS OF NAZARETH: AN UNCOMFORTABLE TRUTH

Few subjects spark as much debate as the physical appearance of Jesus Christ. For centuries, the image of a white, blue-eyed Savior has dominated Christian iconography. But does this portrayal align with historical evidence? The Bible, along with historical accounts from scholars like Josephus and findings from forensic anthropology, suggests otherwise. Jesus was born in the land of Canaan—a region deeply connected to the African continent. The early depictions of

Jesus in the Roman and Russian Catacombs, along with scriptural descriptions, paint a vastly different picture from the Westernized version so often presented.

Through an exploration of ancient texts, historical evidence, and biblical references, this book seeks to restore the truth about Jesus' identity and the broader Black presence in the Bible. The goal is not to rewrite history, but to reclaim it—to tell the story as it was meant to be told.

This book is more than just a collection of historical facts; it's a reclamation of a rich and vibrant past. It's about weaving the missing threads back into the grand tapestry of human history, celebrating the undeniable contributions of Africans on a global scale, long before the dark chapter of slavery began.

The Bible is Black History is more than just a study of scripture; it is a journey into a past that has been deliberately obscured. By bringing these truths to light, we challenge misconceptions, inspire a deeper faith, and empower future generations to see themselves reflected in the sacred texts that have guided humanity for centuries. This is an invitation to rediscover the Bible through a new lens— one that recognizes and celebrates the undeniable truth: Biblical history is, in fact, Black history. Get ready to embark on a thrilling voyage of discovery, one that redefines Black history and deepens our understanding of the Bible, revealing a past brimming with accomplishment, resilience, and cultural richness.

Written by Ife B. Grady

Part One:
ANCIENT AFRICANS IN EARLY AMERICA

I must tell my story because it is different from the story told about me.

CHAPTER ONE

African Presence in Prehistoric America

THE TRUTH ABOUT CHRISTOPHER COLUMBUS

You can always tell the soundness of a truth by the army of lies that surround and protect it from being revealed. My job is to lay siege to that army.

Were Africans part of the welcoming committee when Christopher Columbus arrived in the New World?

On Columbus' second voyage, he landed in Hispaniola (present-day Haiti). The natives told him that Black men came from across the sea trading in gold-tipped spears. Columbus collected a few of these spears and took them to Spain for analysis. Their composition was determined to be eight parts gold, six parts silver, and eight parts copper. This was the exact metal composition in Guinean spears.

On his four voyages, Columbus stopped at the following Caribbean locations: the Bahamas, Cuba, Puerto Rico, Haiti,

Dominica, Trinidad, Jamaica, and Panama. At these landings, he met at least three Black African groups: the Black Caribs, the Taino, and the Arawak. The first two are subgroups of the Arawak.

As quiet as it is kept, Columbus never landed on North or South American soil. The shoreline of South America was visible to him when he landed in Trinidad, however, for whatever reason, he chose not to venture forth. So, in light of that, why do people say that Columbus discovered America, and what does "discovered America" mean anyway?

In the early 1400s, before the voyages of Columbus, the Portuguese made several trips to the southwestern coast of Africa. While there, they witnessed large African ships, loaded with merchandise, set sail westward across the Atlantic toward the Americas. The Portuguese had no knowledge of these merchant ships' destination because no European had ever traversed the Atlantic Ocean.

WHO IS NOT—BUT SHOULD BE—RECOGNIZED AS THE PERSON WHO STARTED THE TRANS-ATLANTIC SLAVE TRADE?

According to Spanish historians, Columbus ordered 1,500 men and women seized from the black Arawak tribes in the Bahamas. Four hundred were ultimately released, five hundred were sent to Spain, and six hundred were enslaved by settlers Columbus left behind on the island. About 2/5th of those on the voyage to Spain died before reaching their destination and were unceremoniously tossed overboard.

I have a confession to make, and this seems to be a good place to make it. None of the groundbreaking historical revelations in this book was the result of any original research on my part.

Being somewhat lazy, all I did was go on a treasure hunt. The treasure I sought was the gold mine of historical truths embedded in the many books and publications published by our black scholars over the decades. Unfortunately, the majority of these writings suffered from media non-exposure.

CHAPTER TWO

Pre-Columbian Presence of Africans in Early America

At least three African groups existed in North America before the arrival of Columbus, the Christian era, and even before the arrival of the Native Americans: the Washitaw Nation, the Yamasees, and the Black Californians (or Mojaves). There were also prehistoric African groups south of the border: the Afro-Dariente of Panama, the Garafundas on the island of St. Vincent, and the Choco of Columbia. Finally, according to Brazilian scientists, a very ancient group of Africans arrived in Brazil around 30,000 BC. To repeat: according to Brazilian scientists, a very ancient group of Africans arrived in Brazil around 30,000 BC.

The largest and most significant pre-historic African nation in the continental US was the Washitaw Nation. As indicated above, they were in North America before Columbus, the birth of Christ, and thousands of years before the Native Americans.

This Nation of Africans controlled a vast area of North America that was approximately one million square miles and included all or parts of what are now Louisiana, Texas, Oklahoma, Mississippi, and Arkansas.

According to the Washitaw, when the Spanish claimed dominance over the Louisiana Territory, they excluded the land belonging to the Washitaw Nation. Similarly, when the French defeated the Spanish to claim the Louisiana Territory, they, too, excluded Washitaw land.

Is there any concrete evidence to support the existence of the Washitaw in ancient America?

Skeletons found in Washitaw gravesites from the pre-Columbian period show tall people with characteristic African features. These gravesites were carbon dated at 10,000 BC. Let's not lose sight of the significance of what I just said; archeologists found skeletons of tall black people in the US that date back to 10,000 BC.

The Washitaw say they are descendants of pre-historic African seafarers who settled in North America thousands of years ago. These ancestors were builders of boats and earthen mounds.

The Washitaw are called "Mound Builders" because they built hundreds of earthen mounds of varying shapes all over the southern and midwestern United States. Some took the shape of pyramids while others the form of animals or birds. The mounds, in addition to providing shelter in cold climates, were used to facilitate worship and the burial of honored dead.

Being Black, many of the tribe became the targets of slave hunters and, thus, victims of the slave system. However, the Washitaw survived the holocaust of slavery intact and maintained their identity as a separate independent nation.

THIS IS GOING TO BLOW YOUR MIND!

In 1991, the US Congress passed a law that resulted in the return of 68,000 square miles of stolen land back to the black Washitaw Nation. It was signed by Papa Bush. What makes this action so astonishing is that, for centuries, the US government stole and appropriated native lands without bothering to offer any compensation. There are very few if any documented cases where stolen Native lands were returned to their rightful owners.

In 1993, The United Nations Center for Human Rights recognized the black Washitaw empire as "the oldest aboriginal group of people on earth."

The Washitaw Nation continues to exist, and today you can visit their most sacred site: the great Bird Mound located at Poverty Point in the village of Pioneer, LA, near Monroe. In prehistoric times, this Bird Mound Complex functioned as a cultural center and temple. Scientists place its date of origin at approximately 2000 BC. 2000 BC is 3492 years before the arrival of Columbus. Can you calculate how I arrived at this number? (2000+1492=3492)

Recently, an ancient African community (not the Washitaw) dated 10,000 BC was found in North Louisiana, clearly confirming that people of color were in the region then.

Thus, we have irrefutable scientific evidence that Africans were in North America for thousands of years before the arrival of the Europeans and even before the arrival of the Native Americans, and some of these original Black Native American groups are still here.

From where do you think the first enslaved Africans in the US came?

The evidence is undeniable that the first Africans to be enslaved in America did not come from Africa but from the Black Native American tribes. These tribes, however, did not accept enslavement without a fight: they engaged the British, Spanish, and Americans in fierce battles and bloody wars. While most Black tribes were ultimately defeated, the message was clear: efforts to force them into slavery would come at a high price. The hills still echoed with the footsteps of their ancestors, and neighboring tribes were brothers with whom they had shared bread and blood.

It was at this point that slave traders turned to Africa to obtain people for enslavement. They reasoned that people brought to a strange land, where a strange language was spoken, would be more easily controlled and less likely to become runaways.

For those of you who are still skeptical, I recommend reading *The First Americans Were Africans* by Professor David Imhotep.

The Yamasee Wars of 1711 and 1715

The Yamasee tribe was one of the black American tribes in the continental US for thousands of years before those we now consider Native Americans.

Somewhere in the Southeastern US, around the year 1711, the black Chief of the Yamasee nation became enraged at the latest intrusion into their tribal land by nearby British settlers. Meetings and discussions with settlers always resulted in broken promises and sincerely uttered lies. Something had to be done to stop the relentless encroachments on their land. The chief stepped out of his tent and called for an Elder; he instructed that Elder to call an urgent meeting of the Council of Elders.

When the Elders were assembled, the chief joined them and started pacing with a lowered head, mumbling to himself. Coming to a stop in front of a senior elder, he raised his head and questioned the group, "Are we nothing? Have we no honor?" No one stirred and no one responded. He resumed his pacing. Finally, he stopped in front of the same elder. This time he looked directly at him and said, "Do you not care that the land of our ancestors is being stolen? Are we like prairie dogs who run for a hole when faced with danger?"

Finally, the chief sat in the middle of the group and asked for their council. "What can we do?" asked one Elder. "They have many more weapons than we do."

Another, looked up from making marks in the dirt and thoughtfully asked, "Will we allow the stench of our silence to offend the nostrils of our ancestors? We must take back what is ours."

A third responded, "Is honor more important than defeat? If we lose, we lose more than land."

Feeling the weight of this difficult decision, the chief looked up and once again addressed the council. "Yes," he said, "Honor is more important than defeat. Do you think the thieves will take less if our mouths remain closed and our weapons idle? Our ancestors have been on this land since the time of ice. It will sadden their hearts to see that we quarrel over whether we should protect and defend the land that they left to us, the land that they loved and fought for."

Finally, the chief stood up and raised his ceremonial spear, signaling that he had reached a decision. He plunged the spear into the ground with such force that it made several elders scamper. Looking toward the heavens, he whispered a prayer and then, in a thunderous voice, cried out, "No respect, no honor, no Yamasee. The ancestors have spoken. Prepare the nation for war."

So began the War of 1711 between British settlers and the Yamasee Nation. The settlers, with the support of men from other nearby settlements, were soon victorious. But instead of taking Yamasee land, they seized their women and children, took them to slave markets, and presented them for sale. This merciless, painful act so enraged the Yamasee men that they began to prepare for what became a bloody war.

The Yamasee Uprising of 1715

The Yamasee were generally thought of as gentle people. However, they were also known to be fierce warriors in battle.

They began to organize what could only be described as a massive Pan-Indian Army. It was a coalition of some fourteen black and white tribes. In the book *The Yamasee War*, William Ramsey wrote, "Warriors from virtually every nation in the South joined together in one of the most potent Native coalitions ever to oppose the British in colonial North America." This Pan-Indian Army was by far the largest army formed on US soil prior to the War of Independence.

According to Ramsey, on April 15, 1715, the predominantly black native army attacked and killed ninety white slave traders and their families. The local settlers were caught completely off guard. The Yamasee followed the initial strike with a major attack on plantations around Port Royal (near modern-day Beaufort). With the help of other coalition members, they killed one hundred settlers and put the rest into a state of panic.

Soon news of the massacre of slave traders and their families began to filter into greater Charleston. Those not killed hastily abandoned their homes and property and fled the state.

Ramsey records that adding to the fear generated by the assaults on slave traders was the news that the Catawba and Cherokee tribes laid siege to plantations north of Charleston. In May 1715, approximately four hundred Catawba warriors and seventy Cherokee warriors terrorized the northern part of the Charleston settlements. They ambushed the cavalry and killed the entire force of ninety men.

Somewhat later, the same two tribes attacked Fort Shenckingu, killing most of their defenders and capturing the fort.

These frightful events took an enormous psychological toll on the remaining settlers. The very thought of encountering the fury of the Pan-Indian army struck terror into their hearts. As a result, South

Carolina settlers abandoned their homes and farms in droves and sought refuge in other states, mostly North Carolina.

Unfortunately, soon after the success of these early battles, the Cherokee tribe withdrew from the war, which turned out to be the most critical factor affecting the outcome.

An Eye-Witness Account

A Charleston merchant writing to his employer in London described the attack and torture of Native agent Thomas Nairne: "But next morning at dawn, terrible war-whoops were heard, and a great multitude of black Indian warriors was seen whose faces and several other parts of their bodies were painted with red and black streaks, resembling devils out of Hell.... The terrifying physical appearance of the black warriors and their frightening war cries struck fear deep into the souls of the Settlers."

After capturing Agent Nairne, the native warriors bound him tightly to a stake, placed firewood all around him, and set it to burn slowly. The gentle flames caused him to suffer horrible torture for several days.

The settlers were ultimately successful in convincing the Cherokee not to reenter the war. They used all manner of enticements and finally succeeded in keeping them out. Gradually, the settlers began to turn the tide on the battlefield and soon emerged victorious.

April 15, 2024, marked the 309th anniversary of the Yamasee Uprising of 1715. As indicated above, when it ended, over four hundred British settlers were killed, most of whom were slave traders, slave catchers, and their families. Hundreds more fled home and land to escape the fury of the advancing native army. This war, has been described as the bloodiest conflict on US soil prior to the Civil War. After the defeat, a portion of the Yamasee nation migrated south and joined the Seminole Nation.

Why have American Historians been silent on this war?

The reasons are numerous:

1. Our black ancestors came very close to winning the war. The settlers suffered major defeats before ultimately gaining the upper hand. The end of the story might have been quite different had the Cherokee (one of the largest tribes) not dropped out of the conflict.
2. Our Pan-Indian Army put such fear into the hearts of the settlers that they fled for their lives in large numbers. While there is glory in victory, there is no glory in near defeat, no glory in telling the story of how you had to run for your life in the face of a fearsome, formidable foe.
3. The primary lessons learned were that black native tribes could and would fight to protect what was rightfully theirs and attempts to force their people into slavery would come at a very high price.

There is nothing in these painful lessons that American historians would want to write history books about.

CHAPTER THREE

The Grand Canyon

Now I'm going to tell you a story of intrigue and fascination. You have my permission to sit at the edge of your seats.

What would you think if I told you that ancient black Egyptians came to the Grand Canyon and settled there for years?

On April 5, 1909, an article appeared in the *Phoenix Gazette* in Arizona reporting on an archeological find in the Grand Canyon under the leadership of archeologists G.E. Kincaid and S.A. Jordan and sponsored by the Smithsonian Institute. The expedition discovered a massive man-made tunnel network that went deep into the side of a high cliff and extended for miles underground.

Today, the entrance to this tunnel system is nearly inaccessible. It is three hundred and ninety-five feet above the current level of the Colorado River. The tunnel is located approximately 1,000 feet below the surface and expands for miles underground. All areas of this tunnel complex were ventilated. What does this tell you? It suggests that the builders of this massive tunnel possessed advanced engineering know-how.

It was reported that this expansive underground complex, carved out of a steep mountainside, could accommodate up to 1,000 residents.

There is a gold statue of an Egyptian king situated at the entrance to the main chamber. The statue seems to be that of an Oriental monarch, seated in the traditional crossed-legged style. The eyes of the statue also appear to be monolid, a shape commonly seen in people of Asian descent. However, written at the base of the statue is the name *Khufu*. Khufu was an Egyptian pharaoh who reigned around the year 2500 BC.

You need to be aware that not all Africans look alike. The Bushmen of the Kalahari, one of the most ancient tribes in Africa (also called the San Kon people) have, what we might call "oriental eyes." However, they had those eyes for thousands of years before the emergence of the Chinese.

Back to the main Chamber of this enormous tunnel network. This Chamber is twelve feet wide and, radiating from it like the spokes of a wheel, were thirteen passageways arranged in an exact geometric pattern. Radiocarbon dating places the age and construction of the tunnel network at around the year 1700 BC.

The construction of a tunnel network with such skillful engineering was unquestionably the work of an advanced prehistoric civilization. What civilization could that have been in mid-America around the year 1700 BC?

The evidence is overwhelming that the race that built and inhabited this mysterious cavern was Black Egyptian. Some of the artifacts found in the cave included: Egyptian statues, war weapons, copper instruments, and boomerangs. Egyptian hieroglyphic writing was observed on tablets and on some of the walls.

However, the most startling and dramatic discovery was in one of the larger rooms at the end of one of the thirteen passageways.

Here was found a crypt, a burial room filled with mummies of Black Africans, each mummy (according to archeologist Kincaid) measured nine feet tall and each was situated on its own little platform. They were arrayed on the walls around the room in a neat pattern and at three different levels. Carbon dating places the age of the mummies at around 1600 BC. At that time, there were no Native American tribes or groups that practiced mummification.

To reiterate, mummies of Black Africans were found in the Grand Canyon as far back as 1600 BC.

The questions that cry out for answers at this time are when, how, and why did the Africans come to this region of the US—and why did they leave?

The artifacts found in this massive tunnel network were identical to artifacts found in Africa; none resembled artifacts known to be the work of any tribe in the Americas.

From the mountains of the Grand Canyon, the Egyptians extracted gold, silver, and copper. Scientists found many ruins of Egyptian-styled metal smelters and furnaces in the Grand Canyon. (The smelting process uses heat and chemical-reducing agents to decompose ore and other unwanted elements, leaving pure refined precious metal.)

NOW THINGS START TO GET STRANGE!

The Smithsonian Institute, which sponsored and funded the project in 1909, now claims to have no knowledge of the expedition, its discoveries, nor the scientists whom they hired to conduct the expedition. Anyone contacting the Smithsonian in search of information about this historic find will be told there are "no records found." They have destroyed all records of the event and, as far as they are concerned, it never happened.

Notwithstanding the above denial, the Smithsonian has displayed several artifacts from this site at its Institute.

It gets even stranger!

The entrance to the tunnel system is now completely sealed off and carefully guarded. Who do you think sealed it off and who guards it? FBI agents. Neither explorers nor visitors are permitted to enter. In fact, they are so concerned about what might be found in this cave that they sealed off access to it and every other man-made cave in the Grand Canyon. (Yes, there were other man-made caves in the Grand Canyon with Egyptian artifacts and writing.)

There are also numerous Egyptian-style pyramids located in the Grand Canyon but, unlike those built in Egypt and Nubia, the pyramids in the Grand Canyon were carved out of the tops of high cliffs.

The evidence is incontrovertible that black Egyptians did in fact visit the Grand Canyon and that their sojourn was not a brief one.

CHAPTER FOUR

The Mystery City of Cahokia

I'm going to invite you to listen carefully as I describe an ancient American city that flourished 400 years before the arrival of Columbus. This city was a large cosmopolitan center with a population of 20,000, which was larger than the population of London at that time. It was unearthed from under the present-day cities of St. Louis, Missouri and East St. Louis, Illinois.

Pay close attention, and as you listen to the incredible facts about this amazing city, I want you to think about just who the people were who built, occupied, and governed this magnificent ancient city in the good old USA.

As you read, I'm going to give you clues to write down. This will help you in determining what group built Cahokia.

Imagine, if you will, the sudden and unexpected discovery of an ancient American city that was a major population center around the year 1050 AD, four hundred years before Columbus. (Write *four hundred years before Columbus.*)

The city was named Cahokia after a local native tribe. This cosmopolitan city in its heyday boasted an impressive population of

15,000–20,000 within the confines of the city and another 20,000 in the surrounding areas. (Write *population 20,000.*) French Monks were the first Europeans to enter the area in the mid-1700s. The sight of a magnificent pyramid completely captivated them. They named the pyramid Monks Mound. Modern archeologists, however, did not get around to excavating the city until 1921.

It can be easily understood why there was very little information about this sprawling city prior to its discovery. It lay hidden beneath the modern city of St. Louis for a thousand years. The city limits extended across both sides of the Mississippi River (including what is now East St. Louis). At that time, it was the most sophisticated urban center in ancient North America. For upwards of one hundred years, Cahokia was the cultural center of the Western Hemisphere. Its influence could be observed in areas as distant as Minnesota and Florida.

Anthropologists were amazed when they realized that this newly unearthed cosmopolitan city was carefully laid out by skilled urban planners quite knowledgeable in the unique design of large urban municipalities.

What is an urban planner? It is someone who plans and designs the layout of large complex cities. It was obvious to even the most casual observer that this city did not just happen; it was planned. It was built on a typical urban grid system with an enormous pyramid as its centerpiece. A grid system is the planned layout of a city's streets, traffic patterns, homes, business districts, pedestrian plazas, etc. (Write *built by skilled urban planners.*)

As would be expected from a large, broad-based population center, the inhabitants included government officials, religious leaders, scientists, astronomers, skilled tradesmen, and artisans.

Downtown Cahokia featured a town center and broad pedestrian plazas. (Write *had a town center and pedestrian plazas.*) Sacred buildings and the homes of civic leaders were set atop vast earthen mounds. Also built on the top some of these mounds were temples where the bones of former leaders and sacred ancestors were interred.

Apparently, Cahokia was not immune to attacks from hostile neighbors. As a deterrent, they built a high stockade wall that surrounded the entire city with guard towers located every seventy feet. This wall enclosed the Monks Mound pyramid, five hundred thatch-roof houses, and some one hundred and twenty earthen mounds. (Write *120 Earthen Mounds in the city.*)

The Cahokians farmed, traded, and hunted. However, corn was the city's staple and its dominant economic commodity.

Ornamental beads were used to facilitate trade and personal business exchanges. Beads were also collected as a sign of wealth. The more valuable ornaments were passed down from generation to generation. Positions of power and prestige in the city were passed down as an inheritance or a birthright.

As indicated above, a unique feature of this city is the location of one hundred and twenty earthen mounds of varying sizes within the city limits. This is the largest concentration of earthen mounds in one location in the Western Hemisphere. Some of these mounds were constructed entirely of clay and mud, while others had a foundation of stone. Many of the stone mounds had caves carved out beneath them and buildings built on top of them. (Write *caves built under earthen mounds.*)

If you were to view Cahokia from above, your attention would be immediately drawn to a regal pyramid that dominated the landscape.

Monks Mound is impressive from whatever position it is being viewed. It is by far the largest archeological site in the continental US today. On a clear day, you can see the St. Louis Arch from the top of Monks Mound. (Write *a large pyramid in the middle of the city*)

The Cahokians developed a yearly calendar. This calendar consisted of many wooden poles erected in the ground and arranged in a perfect circle. The time of year was determined by the way sunlight appeared between the poles. The poles were so aligned with the Earth and the Sun so as to accurately indicate when the four seasons began. On the first day of each season, the sun would line up with a specific pole in the circle, alerting farmers as to when to plant and harvest. Scientists dubbed this calendar "Woodhenge." (Write *constructed an accurate calendar.*)

You should have written down the following:

- 400 years before Columbus
- Population 20,000
- Built by skilled Urban Planners
- Had a Town Center and Pedestrian Plazas
- 120 Earthen Mounds in the city
- Caves built under Earthen Mounds
- A large pyramid in the middle of the city
- Constructed an accurate calendar

Now we've come to decision time. Who built Cahokia? Which of the following groups do you think is responsible for building this great urban city of Cahokia?

1. Native Americans
2. Europeans
3. Asians
4. Africans
5. Others (If so, who?)

Select one of these five and justify your choice based on the facts you have just written down.

Native Americans

Historians and anthropologists are united in the belief that this amazing city was built and inhabited by Native Americans. If you were to Google Cahokia on the internet, virtually every listing would confirm to you that this city was built and dominated by affluent Native Americans.

Historians marveled at the fact that Native Americans who had probably never seen a city of this dimension somehow planned and built one.

Let's have a closer look at the evidence:

1. There were many tribes that lived in the area where Cahokia was found. In fact, the city was named after a local native tribe, but that tribe did not build Cahokia.
2. To date, no tribe has stepped forward to claim Cahokia as their ancestral home.
3. There is no evidence that, in 1050 AD, the Native Americans had developed the urban planning know-how sufficient enough to lay out and build a cosmopolitan city. If they were capable of planning and building large cities, where are some of their other cities?
4. The scientists writing on the internet did not produce any evidence that Native Americans were knowledgeable in building large stone structures, such as government buildings or multi-level temples. On TV and in the movies, all you see Native Americans build are teepees and some wooden structures.

5. Native American tribes at no time had a history of erecting pyramids or constructing complex earthen mounds.
6. Native Americans did not, nor do they now, build protective walls around their villages or reservations.
7. Finally, Native American traditions do not reveal any working knowledge of the positions or movement of heavenly bodies. This knowledge is essential if one is to construct an accurate calendar.

Europeans

There is nothing about Cahokia construction that would suggest it is a European city. Europeans in that day were not known to build thatch-roof houses, temples atop huge earthen mounds, or pyramids.

Question: who was the first European to come to the New World? Columbus.

If Cahokia was built 400 years before Columbus, Europeans could not have built it.

Asians

There is no documented evidence of a large group of Asians living in Middle America around the year 1050 AD.

Asians have no history of building earthen mounds within their cities (or anywhere else for that matter).

The construction of peasant homes within Asian cities at that time differed significantly from the construction of thatch-roof homes built at Cahokia.

There is no evidence that Asians built pyramids at any time. Today, there are over a hundred pyramids in China, and they do not know how they got there or who put them there.

Africans

Now let's have a look at the possibility that it was Africans (or their descendants) who built this magnificent city.

From previous studies, we know that Africans were in the US before Columbus and even before the Native Americans.

Africans were certainly capable of building and managing large, culturally sophisticated cities. Many of their cities were built years before the birth of Christ and many still exist:

1. Memphis, Egypt, est. population 60,000, 3100 BC
2. Alexandria, Egypt, est. population 300,000, 331BC
3. Carthage, Tunisia, est. population 500,000, 818BC.
4. Timbuktu, Mali, est. population 54,000, 1100 AD. (This city flourished around the same time as Cahokia.)

The Africans built many magnificent stone structures, including buildings and massive sculptures of people and animals. The Sphinx and the pyramids are good examples. Continental Africans have a long tradition of building mounds, and they carried that tradition to many parts of the world.

There was no history of pyramid-building anywhere in the world before the arrival of Africans. Almost everywhere they explored in antiquity, the Africans built pyramids: in China, Mexico, Turkey, Iran, Indonesia, France, Italy, Cambodia, the US, etc. Many are still in existence.

The Africans had a superior working knowledge of the stars and the movement of heavenly bodies. They used this knowledge to establish trade routes around the world. They navigated the oceans using the nighttime positioning of the stars and the daytime positioning of the sun.

Over thousands of years, Africans developed many calendars. One calendar of Black Egyptian origin was imported to Mexico around 1500 BC and had a start date of 3113 BC and an end date of 2012 AD.

Then by process of deduction and elimination, we must conclude that the only group in the US in 1050 AD with the know-how to plan, build, and manage a metropolis like Cahokia is the Africans.

Postscript: Mound 72

In a cave beneath a large mound located in the city known as Mound 72, researchers found a burial site that included the skeletal remains of 280 individuals.

There is something very telling about the statistic (280 complete skeletons) that is not immediately obvious. Consider the following account of an ancient skull found in Brazil: craniologists and archeologists who examined this skull were able to determine that it belonged to a Black female, was 12,000 years old, and came from continental Africa.

If Brazilian scientists could obtain so much vital information from a single skull, why is it that scientists and archeologists at Cahokia with 280 complete skeletal remains at their disposal could continue to claim, with a unanimous voice, that no one knows who the Cahokians were? The truth is not that they do not know to whom these remains belong but that they don't want you to know that all or most of the 280 skeletons are the remains of Black Africans.

If they acknowledge that at least some of these 280 skeletons were the remains of Black Africans, they would have to explain how the Africans got there. Our history books tell us that the first Africans to come to America arrived on a Dutch slave ship in 1619, some 569 years after Cahokia.

Therefore, based on the evidence presented, the only logical conclusion that can be reached is that it was Africans who built and dominated the splendid urban city of Cahokia in the middle of the USA in 1050 AD.

CHAPTER FIVE

Ancient Africans South Of The Border

Take out your smartphones, iPods, tablets, and anything else that has internet access, and look up the Ancient Olmec Civilization. Let's see who can be the first to determine where this civilization took place.

THE OLMEC CIVILIZATION

In 1858, Tres Zaportes, a little-known village in Central Mexico, was the scene of an archeological find of historic proportion. The archeologists searched at this site for information about a prehistoric civilization called the Olmec, or Shi, people, who were known to have flourished in the region around 1500-600 BC (or 3500–2600 years ago).

At the dig, archeologists unearthed an enormous stone head finely carved out of a single basalt rock. This colossal stone head was seven feet high and weighed ten tons. It was skillfully carved with naturalistic perfection and displayed individualistic Black African features: full lips, high cheekbones, a protruding jaw, and a fleshy, wide nose. Carbon dating placed the age of this stone head at around 1000 BC.

After publishing a few scientific papers and hosting a few professional seminars, the discovery was largely ignored for eighty-one years. Wild theories emerged to explain the presence and appearance of the stone head, to explain why what you saw was not what you saw, an African face.

There was something special and unique about this stone head at Tres Zaportes, something scientists would not be allowed to reveal for 123 years. Can you guess what that might have been? On the back of this stone head was hair carved into seven African-style cornrows.

Eighty-one years later, in 1938, other expeditions were organized at La Venta, San Lorenzo, and Monte Alban, all of which are in central Mexico. Archeologists unearthed more of these finely carved colossal heads. They were on average 7-9 feet high and weighed 25-40 tons. Each displayed individualistic African features, and each was carved out of a single huge basalt rock. Ultimately, a total of twenty two finely carved African colossal stone heads were unearthed, each with unique African features.

Also found at the digs were hundreds of smaller terracotta figurines and sculptures with distinctly African features, even some with kinky hair and facial scarification such as is only found among certain African tribes.

Who were the Olmecs?

a. Native Mexicans
b. Africans
c. People from other places
d. All of the above

The Olmecs fused cultures from many countries. However, the dominant group was the Africans. They were the leaders, the priest-king class.

La Venta was the capital city of the Olmecs. La Venta was the governmental, religious, and cultural center of the Olmec world. A central feature of this capital city was a large ceremonial plaza, on which was located the following:

- America's first pyramid was on the plaza. It took 800,000 hours and a labor force of 18,000 to build this 110-foot-high pyramid, the largest structure in the Americas at that time. (The authenticity of the 800,000 man-hours and 18,000-sized labor force is somewhat questionable.) This pyramid at La Venta is still there. A question that could be asked is how natives could build a large pyramid when evidence indicates that they had neither seen nor built one before.
- Four colossal stone heads were on the plaza. They were situated at the front, facing the Atlantic Ocean from whence the Africans came. The practice of carving giant images of important personages is one of the most consistent and enduring features of African sculptural tradition.
- Thirty earthen mounds were on the plaza. Africans have been building earthen mounds for thousands of years in Africa. They carried this practice to distant areas around the world where they settled, including Mexico and the continental US.
- Mosaic-paved streets were on the plaza, a unique feature indeed for that period of time.

The Olmec civilization is considered by scientists to be the mother civilization of the Americas. All subsequent civilizations in the Americas were influenced by Olmec practices and traditions. This includes the Mayas, Zapotecs, Aztecs, and Incas. The influence of the Olmec civilization also extended to tribal nations in North America.

Africans who dominated the Olmec elite evidenced a blend of cultures from several African nations: West Africa (probably Mende), Egypt, and Nubia. The evidence of African dominance is both overwhelming and indisputable.

The Evidence

1. Skeletons of Africans have been found in Mexico dating back to the Olmec period.
2. The Olmec priest-kings shared the same race as the Africans, as evidenced by the magnificent detail of the sculpted African heads.
3. The Africans that made up the Olmec must have occupied positions of authority and reverence. No member of nobility or King would allow finely carved colossal sculptures to be made of their peasants or servants without first having them made of himself. Would you?
4. They spoke an African Language (most likely Mende) and used the same script as the Africans. Both Mende script and Egyptian hieroglyphics have been found on monuments in Central Mexico from this period.
5. The Olmec had knowledge of astronomy and mathematics imported from Africa. They knew the Earth was round and revolved around the sun. What did Europeans believe about Earth at that time? Up until the 1700s, they believed it was flat.
6. The Olmecs used a calendar that dated back to exactly 3113 BC. Since it was determined that the Olmecs flourished between 1500 – 600 BC, this calendar, which predates the Olmec by 2000 years, could not have been of their origin. The Egyptian god Bes, an ancient Dwarf God, in the center of this calendar clearly identifies it as Egyptian.
7. The Olmecs built pyramids that were patterned after those built in Egypt and Nubia. The largest ancient Pyramid in Mexico,

Teotihuacan, has the exact dimensions and global positioning as the great pyramid of Gaza in Egypt. There was no history of pyramid-building in the Americas or anywhere else in the world prior to the arrival of Africans.
8. Olmec's religious practices were identical to those of West Africa and Egypt. Both the Olmec and West Africans practiced worship of the planet Venus. Olmec shamans and African priests used similar masks during religious ceremonies and wore robes of royal purple.
9. Most of the colossal stone heads displayed Nubian war helmets.

The takeaway for this section is that there is indisputable evidence that Black people were not only in Central America some 3500 years ago, but they were among the dominant ruling class.

How did the Africans get to the Americas? I'm glad you asked.

Do you think that one of our young adventurous ancestors in Africa could sail to the Americas in a small boat that he and his tribesmen built? Let's have a look!

There are three very strong Atlantic Ocean currents off the west coast of Africa (Ocean currents are rivers within the ocean). One current is off the Cape Verde islands, another off the Senegambia coast, and the third off the lower southwestern coast of Africa. Each would bring even the smallest unsophisticated boat directly to the Americas without much effort. If they could stay afloat, they would make it to the Americas.

Brazilian scientists recently reported that an ancient group of Africans arrived in Brazil around the year 30,000 BC.

Thor Heyerdahl

Let me tell you about Thor Heyerdahl.

Thor Heyerdahl was a Norwegian explorer and adventurer with lots of idle time and spare money. He witnessed debates among archeologists as to whether the ancient Africans could cross the Atlantic in small, crude, reed boats. A reed is a tall, straw-like plant that grows at the edge of rivers and lakes. He decided to use his abundant resources to find out for himself whether such a crossing was possible.

He contacted the Baduma people of Chad who were known to be master boat builders in antiquity. For the right price, the brothers agreed to build him an exact replica of an ancient Egyptian reed boat 45 feet long.

Europeans laughed at Thor and the notion that a boat made with reed could stand up to the rigors of the Atlantic Ocean. They pointed out that if you put a cluster of reeds into water, it would sink. Heyerdahl retorted that if you took a piece of steel from the Queen Mary, England's largest ship at the time, and put it into the water, it, too, would sink. Clearly, it is the construction of the vessel that determines its seaworthiness.

When completed, he took the boat to Morocco and set it on course to the Americas. The boat entered into one of the ocean currents off the western coast of Africa and sailed 2700 miles but missed its target destination, Barbados, by 600 miles due to an inexperienced crew.

Undaunted and with money still no object, Heyerdahl commissioned a second ancient reed boat. This one, also launched from Morocco, traveled 3270 nautical miles and arrived in the port of Barbados in 57 days.

This feat prompted 125 other crazed adventurers to attempt to duplicate Heyerdahl's experiment but with even more primitive vessels. A Nigerian adventurer successfully made the trip from Africa to Central America in a small boat that had neither sail nor oars.

The above accounts confirm that Africans were not only capable of crossing the Atlantic Ocean but were in fact making such crossings for thousands of years.

Ancient African Ships
Did ancient Africans have large, ocean-going vessels?

The Africans were also capable of building and navigating ocean-going ships. They built large boats and ships for thousands of years before the birth of Christ. They traveled both land and sea when there were no other races on the planet. The Egyptians, for example, built large ships (1) to transport merchandise and people up and down the Nile, the longest river in the world, and (2) to crisscross the Sahara.

What do I mean by saying they built ships to crisscross the Sahara?
The Sahara was an enormous inland lake system similar to the Great Lakes in the US for thousands of years before drying up and becoming a Desert. These sea-worthy ships were easily converted into ocean-going vessels fully capable of sailing long distances in tumultuous waters and hostile weather. Evidence of their early voyages can be found in ancient China, India, Greece, Australia, Japan, Hawaii, America, and even Europe. All of these places have documented evidence of the early presence of Africans.

The most telling evidence about ancient African ocean-going ships is found in the Bible.

In Acts 27, the apostle Paul is on a ship with 276 other people. The ship is caught in a ferocious storm and the captain realizes that they need to find land to escape the ravages of the storm. Fortunately, the ship ran aground near land and all of the passengers and crew were saved. In addition to the 276 passengers, the ship had a large cargo of grain. This ship was made by black folks in Alexandria, Egypt around the year 60 AD. These facts confirm a few important things for us:

1. In 60 AD, the Africans had ocean-going vessels.
2. They had ships large enough to accommodate 276 passengers and commercial cargo.
3. They knew how to navigate those ships to desired destinations.

Just to give you an idea of the size of some of these ships, in the 1300s (and before Columbus), African merchants delivered several adult elephants on one ship to the emperor of China as a gift.

Although they won't say or print it, European and American scientists are finding it more and more difficult to keep up the myth that they were the first masters of the high seas.

What navigational techniques or devices did the ancient Africans use?

First, let us have a look at the navigational skills of Columbus. Columbus himself wrote that he and his sailors "were like blind men. Although there were eight or nine pilots on board, none of them knew where they were when they had lost sight of land for several days. Our ignorant pilots know not where they are. They would not be able to find the countries again which I have discovered."

Early in their history, the Africans learned to navigate the open seas using the nighttime positioning of the stars and the daytime positioning of the Sun. This knowledge helped them establish and maintain a worldwide trade network thousands of years before the emergence of the Europeans and Chinese. It also helped them navigate the desert after the Sahara dried up.

Part Two

ANCIENT AFRICANS AROUND THE WORLD

CHAPTER SIX

Ancient Egypt's 3,000 Years Of World Dominance

Before we go any further into prehistorical Africans' presence, we must go back to Africa, where it all began.

THE EGYPTIANS

Today I'm going to take you on a journey into ancient Egypt. The ancient Egyptian civilization is recognized worldwide as one of the greatest and longest-lasting civilizations in the world. Its dominance and preeminence lasted over three thousand years. The mighty Roman Empire, by contrast, reigned supreme in Europe for only 500 years.

Where is Egypt located on the map?

1. Asia
2. Europe
3. The Middle East
4. Africa *

Today, there looms a question that we need to answer: who were the ancient Egyptians?

In 1974, a UN conference hosted in Cairo, Egypt was held to determine once and for all just who the ancient Egyptians were. Of the twenty international scholars in attendance, including Egyptologists from Egypt, only two were Black: Dr. Cheik Anta Diop, the brilliant scholar from Senegal, and Dr. Theophile Obenga, a noted scholar from the Congo. At the conclusion of the conference, and following rigorous debate, all of the other eighteen scholars agreed with the arguments put forth by the two Black scholars: the ancient Egyptians, the ones who built the pyramids with great precision, who built a splendid prehistoric civilization, and who erected the massive statue of the Sphinx, were indeed Black Africans.

What country's delegation do you think had the most difficulty accepting a Black African origin in Egypt?

The only group at the conference that had objections to the notion that the early Egyptians were Black Africans was the Egyptian delegation. More about that a little later.

The African name for Egypt is Khemit, which means Black people or Black community.

The early Egyptians and their Nubian neighbors to the south had a long and complex relationship. They explored and dominated many nations around the world. Their affiliation was so strong that several noted Egyptian pharaohs were, in fact, Nubians. The Nubian pharaoh of Egypt's 25th Dynasty revitalized the declining Egyptian civilization and unified the upper and lower kingdoms.

Recently, an ancient skeleton of a Black man was found in Egypt. How old would you guess it was? Think thousands!

The earliest human fossil found in Egypt was that of a male Negroid skeleton, which was found near Taha, Egypt. Through carbon dating, the bones revealed an age of around 35,000 BC. Another

Negroid skeleton was found just north of Aswan, Egypt. This one was dated at approximately 20,000 BC, confirming that Black people were in Egypt thousands of years before the building of the first Pyramid (2,630 BC) and the rise of the First Dynasty (around 3,000 BC).

The above data confirms that ancient Egypt was populated and dominated by Black Africans. However, significant portions of the advanced Egypt civilization was borrowed from Nubia, its neighbor to the south. For example, hieroglyphic writing and mummification were innovations of the earlier Nubian civilization and were later adopted by the Egyptians. Therefore, it must be understood that Egypt was not the mother of advanced Africa, but its child.

Before the 18th Century, and before the start of the slave trade era, no one denied that the Egyptians were Black. Herodotus, the great Greek historian, wrote that the ancient Egyptians had "wooly hair and black skin." Also, at that time (300 BC), Egypt's great cities, such as Alexandria, were recognized worldwide as bastions of superior learning and cultural sophistication.

How often do you think the Egyptians today celebrate their African beginnings and heritage?

It is important, to recognize that the people who live in Egypt today are not the people who built the pyramids; neither are they the people who built a powerful pre-historic civilization that reigned supreme for over 3,000 years.

Here's why. More recent history of Egypt Documents is being conquered and dominated by a succession of other nations. The Syrians conquered Egypt in 654 BC, the Persians in 550 BC, the Greeks in 320 BC, the Romans around the birth of Christ, and lastly the Arabs in 630 AD. This means that the Arab occupation of Egypt took place some 5,000 years after the building of the pyramids and the erection of the Sphinx. Is it any wonder, then, that the people of Egypt today refuse to embrace or acknowledge their Black African heritage? They refuse to acknowledge it simply because it is not their heritage.

Could it be that Egypt was not the oldest advanced civilization in Africa?

Research currently underway in the present-day African nation of Sudan (formally called Nubia) has established that many features of the advanced prehistoric Egyptian civilization did not originate in Egypt but were inventions and innovations borrowed from a much earlier civilization in Nubia. The Nubian kingdom of Tar-Seti flourished for thousands of years in Africa prior to the dawn of the Egyptians. Scientific evidence documents the ancient Nubian civilization of Tar-Seti as the oldest to appear anywhere on the planet. It had six progressive dynasties and twelve pharaohs before the dawn of Egypt.

Let's have a closer look at this early Nubian civilization.

In 1960, Prof. Keith Seele led a team of international archaeologists on an excavation project in Egypt, funded by the UN. The objective of the project was to rescue ancient Nubian artifacts from the Aswan Dam construction site before they were destroyed by construction activity. The Aswan Dam was a massive engineering undertaking designed to provide water and electric power to large regions of Egypt. Time was of the essence because the lake that the dam would create would relegate thousand-year-old artifacts to a watery tomb.

The team unearthed what appeared to be a cemetery with 33 tombs. Analysis of the artifacts in these tombs confirmed that it was not an ordinary burial ground, but a royal cemetery. The cemetery was determined to be from the lost kingdom of Ta-Seti. Archeologists recognized many of the artifacts unearthed in these tombs as items adopted by the Egyptians thousands of years later.

What did the Hippies of the '60s use to cover up the smell of marijuana?

A well-preserved incense burner was unearthed. Sculpted images on the face of the incense burner depicted a palace, a crowned king, and the flight of a falcon deity. This same deity was the object of worship later by the Egyptians and Greeks.

Scientists calculate that the world's first pharaohs sat on the throne at Ta-Seti around the year 5900 BC. As mentioned above, there were six progressive dynasties before the decline of this great civilization. Such could only be sustained within an environment of (1) centralized political power, (2) economic stability, and (3) wealth.

Women in this advanced civilization were regarded as equal to men.

The Tar-Seti society was open to women at all levels. Many women were heads of state and high priests. One female pharaoh, Kentake Qalhata, was so powerful that she commanded and oversaw the building of her own pyramid.

Another history-making find at the Ta-Seti excavation site was the discovery of an ancient written script that resembled Egyptian hieroglyphics. Unfortunately, no member of the archeological team at the site was able to decipher it. That would have to wait for later teams of ancient linguistic specialists. Could this script be the first ever written language?

Death saves the day!

While he was alive, Professor Keith Seele would not allow any information about this ground-breaking dig at the Aswan construction site to be published or discussed with the scientific community. Why keep scientists in the dark about this significant scientific discovery? Professor Ivan Van Sertima was convinced that Seele was motivated not to publish the discovery by racism. The archeological treasure found at the Aswan site was not shared with the scientific community until the Lord stepped in and found a better place for Professor Seele. After Seele's death in 1971, his Afro-American associate, Dr. Bruce Williams, was entrusted with responsibility for completing the project and sharing its findings with the scientific community.

Stolen Legacy

How many of you have ever heard of the Greek philosophers Plato, Socrates, and Aristotle? What would your reaction be if I were to tell you that Greek philosophy did not originate in Greece?

According to Black Professor George G.M. James, author of the book *Stolen Legacy*, "Greek Philosophy is by no means Greek, but Egyptian philosophy." At that time (around 300 BC), Black Egyptians were the most educated and culturally sophisticated people in the world. The Greeks realized this and traveled to Egypt to study.

The Egyptian Mystery System is where higher education took place. The Mystery System was also an Order of Secrecy. Students were required to take a pledge of secrecy before being accepted. As part of that secrecy, students were forbidden to write down anything that they had been taught. Learned Egyptian High Priests were their instructors.

Greeks flocked to Egypt in massive numbers!

Thousands of Greek scholars traveled to Egypt to study under Black Egyptian masters. It's been said that if one were to write a book of a thousand pages, one could not list all of the Greek scholars who went to Egypt to study. These Greek scholars did not attempt to hide the fact that they went to Egypt to receive higher education. Quite the contrary! They viewed this education as a badge of prestige and a point of pride.

The most esteemed Greek philosophers, scientists, and thinkers (Pythagoras, Plato, Socrates, and Aristotle) acquired their "Greek philosophies and scientific knowledge" from learned Black Egyptians. Both Plato and Pythagoras acknowledged in their writings that they and other Greek scholars acquired their advanced knowledge from Egyptian High Priests. The renowned Greek historian Herodotus observed that, whether he was in Greece or Egypt, there was a belief that Greek civilization was a child of the Nile—that is to say, a child of Egypt.

Aristotle was with Alexander the Great when he conquered and sacked the highly advanced cosmopolitan Egyptian city of Alexandria. Before Alexander gave the order to put the torch to the city's magnificent libraries, Aristotle liberated hundreds of books (on a wide range of subjects) and took them back to Greece. These became source material for the schools that he would later establish and reference material for the staggering number of subjects in which he would later claim to be an expert.

What kind of a reception did these Egyptian-trained Greek scholars receive when they returned home?

Not a good one. Greek intelligentsia, political authorities, and religious leaders in Athens universally rejected the ideas of these Egyptian-trained Greek scholars. The problem was that the instruction that the Greeks received from their Egyptian masters emphasized perspectives, cultures, and religious concepts that were foreign to the Greek elite. Therefore, instead of celebrating these Egyptian-trained scholars, they persecuted them.

- Pythagoras was expelled to Italy.
- Socrates was condemned to death and committed suicide in prison.

- Plato was sold into slavery.
- Aristotle was indicted and exiled to a far-off Greek island, Euboea.

What was the reaction of American and European historians to the message of the book *Stolen Legacy*? The publication of *Stolen Legacy* was met with a firestorm of outrage and hostility from white historians. They were offended by the audacity of this Black man and his challenge to the authenticity of their Greek heroes. In addition to a landslide of negative criticism, there was almost instantaneous censorship. The book was published in 1954, and in 1967 I could not find a copy of *Stolen Legacy* in any bookstore in NYC (and there are lots of bookstores in NYC). I partnered with a couple of Muslim brothers and ordered bootleg copies of the book from the country of Jordan. The book is no longer censored and is now widely available on Amazon, but that was not the case in 1967.

Professor George G.M. James died on June 30, 1956, under highly suspicious circumstances, just two years after the publication of *Stolen Legacy*. To this day, it is widely believed that Professor James was assassinated. I am among those who hold to that belief. The book *Stolen Legacy* by Professor James is a must-read for seekers of the truth.

From Superiority to Inferiority

For this section, I need you to pay close attention, because it is here that the concept of African inferiority may have first emerged. During the Dark Ages, Europe descended into near barbarism. There were weak kings, frequent wars, virtually no urban life, and almost universal poverty. As Europe slowly emerged out of the Dark Ages, their non-Greek scholars began to cast about looking for European heroes to support their growing sense of pride. The same Greek scholars who were rejected by the Greek elite were dug up and held as examples of brilliant, innovative Europeans.

This manipulation of history gave birth to a movement to ignore and/or deny the African origin of Greek philosophy. The impact of this "big lie" was to boost their sagging egos and to make them feel superior to non-European people. Unfortunately, it also ushered in the proliferation of African inferiority theories that persist to this day.

CHAPTER SEVEN

Ancient Africans in Early China

Today there is universal acceptance among scientists that Africa is the birthplace of man.

It all started in the Motherland! Within the span of a couple of decades or so, the idea that the human race evolved in Africa hundreds of thousands of years ago went from fringe theory to mainstream thinking. There is universal acceptance among scientists the world over that Africa is the birthplace of humanity, the cradle of civilization, the place where it all started.

The so-called "Out of Africa" theory enjoys rare scientific consensus and is grounded in the results of prestigious historical and DNA studies, all of which report similar findings: that modern humans are all descended from people who first appeared in Africa. Around 60,000-80,000 BC, Africans began to migrate out of Africa by land and sea to other parts of the world.

What do you think was the cause of this great migration?
There is considerable uncertainty and disagreement among anthropologists as to what motivated the Africans to begin to leave

the motherland. Many theories were put forth, but the one I find most compelling is the theory that the sudden cooling of the Earth's climate as a result of the advancing Ice Age prompted migration. This invasion of cold air into the region made life very difficult and uncomfortable for people whose entire life experience had been the sweltering heat of a tropical climate. The migration and the extreme drop in temperatures resulted in a sharp reduction in the population of Africa during that era.

One group of ancient Africans that left Africa around this time migrated to China. Is there any documented historical or cultural evidence of an African footprint in Ancient China?

Africans established many civilizations in China. The two major Black civilizations in early China were the Xia civilization (2205-1766BC) and the Shang civilization (1700—1050 BC)

The Africans who founded the first civilizations in China were described by locals at the time as people with "black and oily skin." These early Africans were said to be small in stature and have slanted eyes, which today is the most identifiable trait of Asians. You need to be aware that not all Africans look alike. There are several groups in Africa that are diminutive in stature and have slanted eyes. One such group is the Kong San bushman of the Kalahari in southern Africa. However, they had those eyes for thousands of years before the emergence of the Asians.

THE XIA CIVILIZATION (2205-1766 BC)

Today we are going to explore an ancient Chinese civilization that emerged from the depths of mythology to the heights of historical significance.

The Xia (She-ya) was the first Black civilization established in ancient China. It flourished between 2206 to 1766 BC and had 17 dynastic kings and 13 generations. As mentioned earlier, it was one of two civilizations established by Africans in ancient China.

For many years, accounts of a Xia civilization was thought to be a myth or a legend. There was no tangible archaeological evidence of its existence until 1959. The Xia civilization now enjoys a permanent place in ancient Chinese history. However, ordinary people in China today are completely clueless about the African contribution to their history.

There is significant historical evidence that the founders of the Xia and the later Shang civilizations came by way of land from Africa through Iran. Some Africans also arrived by sea. They settled along the banks of the Yellow River and were called "Li min." Li min means "black head people." Yes, contrary to volumes of misdirected and forgotten history, Black folks were prominent in ancient China. You might be surprised to know that the oldest skeletal remains found anywhere in China were the bones of Black Africans.

In 1959, China began an excavation project in the ancient town of Erlitou. They were searching for concrete evidence to confirm the existence of the legendary Xia civilization. The excavation at Erlitou succeeded in uncovering the capital city of the Xia dynasty. They found the remains of two palaces, residential areas, royal tombs, well-paved roads, and workshops. They also unearthed cultural relics such as bronze tools, pottery, and work tools made of stone and shell.

In addition to the site at Erlitou, Xia artifacts were also excavated from various other sites: Hernan, Shanxi, and Hubei all revealed something about the black people who dominated the country for more than 400 years.

According to Chinese historical records, the Xia dynasty was said to have been founded by "Yu the Great." This black king was celebrated down through the ages as "the king who controlled the waters."

Yu's father initiated several elaborate projects to control the annual flooding of the Yellow River, which had the effect of devastating valuable farm land for months each year. Unfortunately, he met failure at every turn. None of his projects succeeded in taming the raging flood waters.

Upon his death, Yu continued his father's pursuit. In an effort to learn why his father's projects had failed, Yu spent years studying the Yellow River and its flow. He ultimately succeeded in designing an effective flood control system that put an end to the annual damage done to rich farmland. As an added bonus, he developed an irrigation system designed to channel water into farmlands.

The flood control and the irrigation systems allowed the fertile land along the Yellow River to flourish with an abundance of rich year-round crops. The extraordinary success of these projects solidified Yu's place in Chinese history.

Apparently, King Yu was a down-to-earth brother. He was a benevolent ruler and is said to have eaten and slept with the common workers and spent a significant amount of his time personally engaged in the work of dredging the sediment in the river bed. He toiled with the workers for the entire thirteen years that it took to complete the projects.

Yu created the first imperial Chinese dynasty.

A system of dynastic succession was established under his leadership. He was the first king in China to insist that his son succeed him to the throne. Prior to that time, a virtuous man was chosen by nobles to replace a departing or departed ruler. This made Yu the originator of China's first imperial dynasty and, as mentioned earlier, there were 17 dynasties to follow.

The Xia maintained a strong army. Legend has it that they were the first to introduce horsedrawn chariots to that part of the world. This was yet another invention borrowed from the motherland.

To provide a measure of safety and security, the Xia built walled-in cities, which were the first of their kind in China. These cities were called Yi. This innovation, also an import from Africa, proved to be so successful that it became the standard for succeeding dynasties.

Some Xia peasants lived in houses built on the top of mounds (an old African tradition), while others lived in houses made of grass and mud. Agriculture was the primary work and commodity. They produced millet and soybeans and also raised pigs and cattle.

It is conjectured that the Xia probably spoke Mending, an African dialect.

What brought about the decline of the Xia?

1. Conquest by a stronger group
2. Moral decay at the leadership level*
3. A declining economy
4. Internal intrigue

The woman made me do it!

The fall of the Xia Dynasty is blamed on its last king, Jie, who is said to have fallen in love with an evil, beautiful woman and become a tyrant. After he succeeded to the throne, he lived an extravagant lifestyle day and night without any thoughts for the needs of his country or its people. In fact, he brutally oppressed the common people on a daily basis. His tyrannical reign came to an end when his actions so enraged the people that they rose up under the leadership of Tang (the chief of the Shang tribe) and sent Jie into early retirement, or an early grave, thus ushering in the era of the Shang Dynasty.

Notable achievements of the Xia civilization:

1. Controlled and harnessed the flood waters of the Yellow River.
2. Established an effective irrigation system.
3. Built China's first walled-in cities.
4. Created the first succession dynasty.
5. Flourished for about 400 years.
6. Had a strong political system and a strong army.
7. Used horse-drawn chariots for the first time in China.

The Shang Civilization (1700-1040 BC)

How can you turn a myth into an established reality?

Like the Xia before them, the Shang dynasty was originally considered to be a myth although there was mention of them in ancient Chinese manuscripts. In 1920, archaeologists were finally able to provide concrete evidence of the existence of the Shang civilization when they excavated its capital city Anyang. In 1950, an even earlier Shang capital was excavated. The Shang is the first civilization in China where substantial archaeological evidence and an abundance of documentation exist.

For about 500 years, the Shang ruled a large area around the Yellow River. During that time, 30 kings occupied the throne and established 7 different capital cities.

These black Chinese civilizations began along the Yellow River. Here the fertile soil allowed the farmers to cultivate millet, rice, and possibly soybeans as well as domesticate pigs, cattle, sheep, dogs, chickens, and horses.

The government of the Shang was fairly advanced. It was the first civilization in China to have an organized political system, notwithstanding the fact most of the high levels officials were closely related to the King.

What is the best way to preserve the history and achievements of a people or nation? Record it in print! *Black and white saves a hell of a fight.*

The Black Shang Dynasty was the first civilization in ancient China to develop a complex written language. Such an innovation gave them the ability to record historical events and to document dynastic achievements. The sophistication and complexity of this writing system suggests that some form of it may have existed for many years prior to the Shang.

Shang writing consisted of scratches on the bones and the shells of animals, mostly the scapula (shoulder blade) of oxen and the shells of large turtles. They were called Oracle Bones and used originally by Shang kings to predict the future. An ancient king would inscribe his name and the date on the bone along with a question. For example, he might ask, "Will the king have a son?" or "Will we succeed in battle tomorrow?" or "Will the Queen have a headache tonight?" (Just kidding, wanted to see if you were still alert.) He would then heat the bone or shell until it cracked, and then interpret the shape of the crack, which was believed to provide an answer to their question.

The Oracle bones were first discovered by modern pharmacists who, in an effort the make a few quick bucks, were selling the strange, unknown bones as dragon bones. Their pitch was that the dragon bones possessed mysterious healing powers.

It wasn't until 1899 that these strange bones attracted the attention of anthropologists and, by the 1920's, scientists were able to trace the scripted bones back to the Shang Dynasty in China.

The advent of written communication made it possible for the Shang to pursue advanced scientific endeavors. For example, the Oracle script documented and predicted celestial events such as the eclipse of the Sun and the eclipse of the Moon.

Modern Chinese scientists discovered that the Shang script had virtually the same shapes and meaning as contemporary Chinese writing. Therefore, scholars in China today are able to interpret the messages of the ancient Oracle Bones without much difficulty.

What Egyptian rolling weapon of war found its way into ancient China? You've seen it on TV and in the movies many times.

The use of horse-drawn chariots was new to China during this period and was no doubt imported from Egypt by the Africans. The Chariots gave the Shang soldiers an advantage. It allowed them to cover vast distances at great speeds and also acted as a sturdy platform to enhance archery stability and accuracy.

Shang armies expanded the borders of the kingdom. They demanded tribune, seized precious resources from surrounding tribes, and took prisoners of war after successful battles. The prisoners were put to work as slaves or sometimes used as human sacrifices in religious ceremonies.

Technical advances

Technical advances define great societies. Do you think the Black civilizations in ancient China produced any technical innovations?

Sophisticated casting methods increased the use and value of the composite bronze metal. It was an immensely important metal during the Shang period. Bronze was used to make luxury items, beautiful art, and weapons of war. Bronze swords and spearheads were stronger than swords made with other metals used at that time.

In addition to the mastery of bronze craftsmanship, Shang artists also acquired skill in carving stone, especially jade. Beautifully carved jade sculptures and jewelry rapidly soared in popularity and demand for these artistic gems continues to this day.

Apparently, the Chinese were and are fond of raising a particular worm. Shang farmers raised silk worms. Weavers used the silk to produce fine silk cloth and garments. A silk textile industry was created that thrives even to this day. Their work in silk and other woven materials was and is of the highest quality.

Is it possible to create an accurate calendar without knowledge of the heavens?

The Shang's knowledge of the heavens enabled them to create an accurate calendar. This calendar was based on the cycles of the moon. The scientists knew that the lunar year is shorter than the solar year so astronomers were given the task of making periodic adjustments to the calendar to ensure its continued accuracy.

Let's not lose sight of the fact that we are talking about a Black civilization in China some 3700 years ago that had an intimate familiarity with the location and movement of heavenly bodies. By contrast, the Europeans didn't realize that the Earth was round until the 17th century.

Shang religion

The Shang practiced ancestor worship and believed in the afterlife. Oracle Bones were used to communicate with their ancestors.

What fate awaited you if you were the servant of an Egyptian pharaoh who died on the job?

Shang tombs were very similar to the tombs found in Egypt. Both cultures buried servants with their royalty, and the poor servants had no say in the matter. The Shang frequently buried the King's chariot and horse with him as well.

Decline

After a time, the Zhou, a nomadic people, settled near Shang territory and became vassals of the Shang. Eventually, the Zhou became stronger than the Shang, and in about 1040 BC, they defeated the Shang and destroyed their civilization. The Zhou was successful in defeating them because Shang's leadership at that time suffered from moral decay. The Zhou was the first great Mongoloid civilization in China.

Not a single shred of evidence concerning the thousands of years of Black occupation and contribution to contemporary China can be found in any Chinese museum today. As far as they are concerned, these Black civilizations are still myths, intentionally ignoring all of the tangible evidence and abundant documentation.

While in Shanghai, I visited a museum and saw a lot of artwork by Shang civilization artists. There was no hint that this was the work of black artists.

In summary

The imprint of the ancient Black civilizations on China is still discernable today. Some of their achievements are as follows:

1. Created a complex written language
2. Developed innovative casting methods for bronze metal
3. Created a calendar based on the cycles of the moon.
4. Established an organized political system
5. Had expert knowledge of heavenly bodies and their movements.
6. Created a textile industry that continues to produce fine silk garments to this day.
7. Created an artistic industry that produced beautiful jade sculptures and jewelry.
8. Initiated the practice of ancestor worship

We can best honor the memory of these great Black ancestors by telling their stories, especially to our young people. They need to know that our ancestors are great unsung heroes who, for thousands of years, brought peace, knowledge, and civilization everywhere they went.

CHAPTER EIGHT

Chinese Scientist Awakens To A Foundational Truth

Previously, it was revealed that thousands of years ago during the great African migration, one group left the Motherland and voyaged to China. These ancient Africans established China's first two great civilizations.

Chinese professor Kwany Chih Chang is widely regarded as the founding father of Chinese archaeology. In his groundbreaking work on ancient Africans in China he observed, "There is substantial evidence of Black African populations in early China." To be sure, his conclusions were challenged by other Chinese archaeologists. However, when the dust settled, there was substantial universal agreement.

The earliest documented evidence of the presence of Africans in China dates back to around 50,000 years ago. However, the emergence of Black civilizations in China occurred much later: the Xia dynasty (2205-1766 BC) and the Shang dynasty (1700-1040 BC). While this information was somewhat new to white historians, a few Black historians, such as Runoko Rashidi, Ivan Van Sertima, and Clyde Winter spoke out loud and clear about the early African dominance in China, but their observations received little or no recognition from white historians.

Are Chinese scientists today aware of their ancient African ancestors?

The idea that Blacks were the original inhabitants of China was not only poo-pooed by leading Chinese and Western scientists but also by a few Black scientists. In 2005, Professor Jen Li, a Chinese scientist specializing in DNA analysis, conducted a five-year comprehensive study to determine once and for all the true origin of the Chinese people.

Dr. Li's groundbreaking study was carried out by a team of prominent international scientists from China, Russia, India, Brazil, and other countries. The team set about collecting DNA samples from 165 different ethnic groups around the world. In addition, they collected 12,000 DNA samples from individuals in China and India. Their approach was to focus on a single genetic marker that appeared about 310,000 years ago in Africa.

What are Chinese schoolchildren taught about the origin of the Chinese people?

When Professor Li was a child, students in Chinese schools were taught that there was something special about their people, that the Chinese race evolved from Peking Man (an earlier ancestor who walked the earth 400,000 years ago and was not quite human). They were also taught that the Chinese people evolved on the earth separate and apart from all other human groups.

Which of the following describes what Dr. Li's research team actually discovered?

1. The Chinese race evolved from Peking Man, as believed in China for many years.
2. The Chinese people developed independent of all other humans on Earth but at the same time.
3. The Chinese race evolved from ancestors in Africa*
4. The most ancient ancestor of the Chinese were the Neanderthals.

Li fully expected to confirm (1) that the Chinese were ancestors of Pekin Man and (2) that, though they evolved on the earth at the same time, they were independent of all other human groups.

The analysis of the impressive collection of DNA specimens revealed a conclusion that took the entire international team by surprise. The study offered conclusive evidence that all humans alive today (including the Chinese) originated from ancestors living on the continent of Africa, and that we all carry the 310,000-year-old African genetic marker. That African marker appeared without exception in all of the thousands of DNA specimens collected and analyzed by the team. None of the DNA specimens showed any evidence of a Peking Man ancestor.

The researchers went on to firmly establish that modern man appeared on the planet in one location at the same time. Prof. Li's team not only proved that the Chinese people originated in Africa but that the very first inhabitants of China were, in fact, ancient Africans. This concept of a single origin and a single time for all of mankind shattered long-held Chinese beliefs.

Are today's scientists in China leading the charge to embrace their African heritage?

That is a hard question to answer, but there is at least one convert: Dr. Jen Li. After studying the published report issued by the investigative team, a science reporter asked Dr. Li how he felt about the unexpected findings. Surprisingly, rather than being upset or disappointed by the results, Dr. Li was quite calm and accepting. He observed, "After I saw the evidence generated in my own laboratory, I thought we should all be happy because we are not so different from each other and we are very close relatives." He stated further, "Everybody was a descendant of our ancestors in Africa."

CHAPTER NINE

A Tale Of Two Rich African Brothers

Abubakari, the dreamer King

Can you name a King in 1300 AD (183 years before Columbus) who ruled the richest and most powerful Empire in the world? Look to the motherland!

In 1309, Abubakari Keita II ascended to the throne of the black nation of Mali and became the Mansa, or king, of the largest and wealthiest Empire in the known world at that time. Although he was in the enviable position of being the richest and most powerful ruler in the world, he was not a happy monarch. For example, he was frequently discontent and impatient with the routine business of the throne. In the midst of discussions of the throne's business, he would often let his mind drift to reliving a recurring dream that he experienced as a child. In this dream, he would fly off to strange and unfamiliar lands and discover wonderfully exciting things, things that were very different from the world around him in Mali.

Abubakari began to surround himself with the country's elite intelligentsia: scientists, navigators, astronomers, and other scholars from the rich academic environment of Timbuktu. He was hungry to learn about the world beyond Mali. This select group began to ruminate about the unknown world surrounding the ocean and to speculate as to where the ocean ended.

Abubakari spent many idle hours daydreaming about the exciting discoveries he might experience beyond the shores of his homeland. Aside from the educated elite, very few of his countrymen shared his sense of adventure or curiosity about things beyond the shores of Mali. Quite the contrary, they viewed the vastness of the ocean and the lands that lay beyond with fear and trepidation.

After satisfying himself that the security, government, and economy of the Empire were in excellent condition, the king began to put into motion a plan to fulfill his dream. No expense would be spared in the construction of a formidable fleet, adequately supplied and capable of uncovering the mysterious challenges of the ocean.

The Mansa instructed his people to marshal a legion of shipbuilders. Their task was to build 200 master ships and 200 supply ships to accompany them on an exploratory voyage. When the construction of the fleet reached completion, the king summoned the Captains of the ships and gave them the following instruction: "Do not return until you have reached the end of the ocean or you have exhausted your supply of food and water."

The fleet set sail amid high expectations and great fanfare. However, as time passed and the memory of the fleet faded, the king would go down to the shore daily and scan the horizon. For many months, he saw no sign of his fleet and received no word of their plight. The king could find no peace. He became increasingly restless, anxious, and troubled. After what seemed like an eternity, a single ship appeared on the horizon. Abubakari could not contain his excitement and curiosity. He demanded that the ship's captain be brought to him immediately.

Once before the King, the captain related the following story: "When the fleet had sailed for a considerable distance, they came to what seemed like a strong river current in the middle of the ocean. My ship was last. The others sailed forward, but as they entered this strange current, they were quickly controlled by it and soon disappeared. I decided to return home. I do not know what became of them."

You need to be aware that there are three ocean currents off the West coast of Africa. Any one of these three ocean currents will bring even the most unsophisticated boat directly to the Americas.

The disappointing revelation made the king even more determined to confront the mysteries of the ocean. He set about organizing a massive army of workers unlike anything the country had ever witnessed. He set before this massive army **the task of building nothing short of the largest fleet the world had ever seen.** It would dwarf the previous fleet by several orders of magnitude. The king's command was to build no fewer than 2,000 ships: 1,000 master ships and 1,000 ships with supplies and provisions. The Mansa then recruited a cadre of scholars and skilled tradesmen to be part of the ship's company.

Let's speculate: who was the special person that the king would select to lead the massive fleet on this momentous voyage?

1. His brother, Kankan
2. The captain of the ship that returned
3. The Mansa himself
4. The most experienced ship's captain in the land

The King further ordered the outfitting of a special ship to function as the flagship. This was to be his flagship since he intended to personally command this second expedition.

In 1311, Abubakari conferred temporary power of the throne to his brother, Kankan Musa, with the understanding that Kankan was to assume the powers of the throne permanently if, after a reasonable lapse of time, the king did not return. The King willingly gave up power and riches to pursue knowledge and discovery. He didn't know if he would find land or if the ocean just went on forever. The expedition could bring him fortune and fame or lead him and his men to their doom. Whatever the outcome or consequences, it was his destiny, and he could avoid it no longer.

The day finally arrived when all of the construction and preparation of the fleet was completed. The Mansa clothed himself in a brilliant white robe and a jeweled ceremonial turban. He boarded his magnificent flagship with great pomp and ceremony. Standing at the helm, he scanned the massive fleet, then turned his gaze confidently and defiantly at the Atlantic Ocean. Raising his hand for all to see, Abubakari gave the order to launch the expedition.

Which of the following statements actually describes what happened to the fleet?

1. The fleet was reported to have been lost at sea.
2. Nothing was ever heard of the fleet or Abubakari.
3. The fleet landed in a far-off land and never returned.
4. The fleet returned home when they ran out of food and water supplies.

Fast forward to several months later.

It must have been the throbbing sound of drums that attracted a crowd of natives to the shore to witness the spectacle unfolding before them on the distant horizon. As they strained their eyes to focus, they could see a massive number of strange-looking ships approaching. As the drumming grew louder and the fleet drew closer, they could make out a dark figure standing majestically on the top deck of the lead ship.

There was a murmur of excitement as the strange vessels drew near. Native religious leaders had recently told the people to expect a messenger from "the land of the Sun God" this year. The natives began speaking enthusiastic words of praise and worship to their God.

As the magnificently decorated flagship neared the shore, the Mansa, in royal splendor, stood at the helm, surveying the land and the people before him. His jeweled turban and a long white robe glistened in the noonday sun. The brilliance of the robe was in stark contrast to his dark bearded face.

How must Abubakari II have appeared to the natives in South America with his enormous fleet and all its grandeur?

What little evidence exists points to the Mansa landing in the country of Brazil at a place called Recife. Abubakari never returned to Mali but decided instead to explore the vastness of South America. Upon arrival, Abubakari's fleet sailed along the coast until they found rivers like the Orinoco in Venezuela and the Amazon in Brazil, which they used to venture inland. They established Muslim settlements throughout South America. While so doing, Abubakari did not forget his homeland and maintained contact with his brother.

Why do you think the history book makes no mention of Abubakari's arrival in the Americas with 2,000 ships 183 years before Columbus?

Who do you think was the richest man who ever lived?

A widely accepted but little-known truth today is that the richest person who ever lived was the 12th-century ruler of the Empire of Mali. This obscure ruler amassed a fortune estimated at $400 billion in today's money during his reign. This sum outranks his two closest competitors, the Rothschilds at $350 billion and John D. Rockefeller at $340 billion.

The astounding wealth of this empire came from its production and control of more than half the world's gold and salt.

KanKan Musa (Mansa Musa) Ascends to The Throne of Mal as mentioned in the previous section, KanKan Musa received temporary powers to the throne from his brother, Abubakari, when Abubakari embarked on an expedition to explore the outer reaches of the Atlantic Ocean. As instructed, KanKan waited for a year, and when his brother did not return, he assumed permanent powers of the throne and became KanKan Musa or Mansa Musa. Mansa Musa inherited a professionally trained army of 100,000 soldiers from his brother. The men would be used to increase the power and reach of the empire.

His brother made certain that Kankan received the finest education from the most learned men in Timbuktu, the epicenter for excellence in higher education in the world. Mansa Musa was a good student and spoke several languages other than his native Arabic.

He was an exceptionally skillful leader who exhibited unusual skill and compassion in decision making. As an administrator, he demonstrated unusual competence and compassion in interpersonal dealings and negotiations. Truly an exceptional man!

An early priority of the Mansa was to get rid of the large number of bandits that roamed Mali's major roads, robbing travelers and traders. He ordered the bandits to be rounded up and given stiff and lengthy jail time. Once the roads became safe, travel expanded and markets all over Mali began to grow and thrive.

Can you control the production of a mine when you do not know its location?

Although Mans Musa did not know exactly where most of the country's gold mines were located, he was quite familiar with the complex network of families that controlled and operated these mines. He was also aware of how jealously the families guarded the location of their mines. With wisdom worthy of Solomon, Mansa agreed to allow the locations of the mines to remain anonymous as long as the families maintained the production quotas he established.

Adding to the already swollen treasury was income realized from the taxation of trade and the collection of tribunes from conquered territories.

What other commodity at that time traded at a level equal to that of gold and silver?

Salt was in high demand worldwide and Mali was one of the largest producers. The general rate of exchange was an ounce of gold for an ounce of salt.

Traders of salt would load their camels and walk along side of them for many miles. All day long, the men had to keep walking. If they stopped to sit down for even a few minutes, their camels would also sit down and the salt would slide off the camel's backs and unite with the sand below, becoming useless.

What overseas trip did Malcolm X take that changed his life and his thinking about white people?

Being a devout Muslim, Mansa Musa was determined to make a pilgrimage to the city of Mecca as required by the Quran. This pilgrimage is called "the Hajj." He was excited by the prospect of worshiping in the holy city with Muslims from all over the world.

In the second year of his reign, the Mansa gave instructions to begin preparation for the 4,000-mile voyage to Mecca. He was not deterred by the fact that the journey would include long stretches of scorching desert terrain which complicated and delayed the planning process. It was not surprising then that the planning process took two years to complete, which was almost as long as the journey was expected to take.

Before the anticipated departure, Mansa Musa placed his elder son, Maghan, in charge of the empire for the duration of the Hajj.

On a day sanctioned by the religious high council, the Hajj was sanctioned to begin. The Mansa dressed himself in elegant garments and sat upon a magnificent black stallion who was lavishly adorned with an eloquent gold trimmed saddle.

A crowd assembled to witness the breath-taking splendor and stretch of the caravan. Once the caravan started to move, it appeared to be a long glittering snake moving slowly through the landscape.

Can you guess how many people and animals made up the caravan?

The Mansa's personal servants numbered 13,000 in all. Five hundred of them carried ornamental staffs made of gold and walked on the road in front of the Mansa. Behind him were 12,000 well-dressed slaves, each carrying four pounds of gold bars. Hundreds of horses and a long line of camels formed the backbone of the caravan. Eight thousand well-trained soldiers were there to protect and defend the caravan if necessary.

Eighty camels carried nothing but gold—three hundred pounds each. Some of the gold was in the form of gold dust and bars, and some was fashioned into jewelry and goblets.

How much water do you think a camel can drink in ten minutes?

Finding adequate amounts of water was a constant challenge. A thirsty camel can drink about 25 gallons of water in just ten minutes and can live on it for weeks—even months, depending on the weather. A thirsty person, on the other hand, can only drink a few cups of water at a time and will need another drink within a few hours.

The entire 60,000-person caravan was peaceful and respectful towards the communities they passed through. In addition, Mansa left gifts of gold with local leaders and spent generous amounts for the basic necessities which he purchased.

Observers along the way commented on Mansa's great generosity in handing out alms to the poor.

Once in the Sahara Desert, they experienced daytime temperatures in excess of 130 F and nighttime temperatures close to 100 F.

What navigational tools were used to stay on course in the desert?

Skilled desert navigators were able to keep the caravan on course by studying the position of the stars at night and the position of the sun in the day.

At the end of each day's travel, every member of the caravan received an elaborately prepared meal, complements of the Mansa and his large corps of excellent cooks.

Cairo, Egypt

A glimpse of Cairo, Egypt on the horizon filled the caravan with excitement because it signaled the end of the first leg of the long journey to Mecca.

The Cairo of that day was a large, vibrant city with nearly a million inhabitants; this was in addition to the throngs of people who came to the city to study, trade, and visit its superb libraries and mosques.

Everywhere Mansa Musa went during his stay in Cairo, he gave away gold. Cairo streets were virtually littered with gold and the people were delighted. Though well-intentioned, the Mansa's gifts of gold actually caused a dramatic drop in the value of gold in Egypt. As a consequence, Egypt experienced significant inflation which took up to 12 years to correct.

The standoff with Cairo's Sultan

When Mansa Musa arrived at the Egyptian palace to visit the sultan, he was informed that all guests brought before the sultan were expected to kiss the sultan's hand or kiss the ground before his throne.

Although the Mansa was too polite to say so, he knew that his empire was larger and his wealth far greater than the Sultan's. If any hand was to be kissed, thought the Mansa, it should be his. Thus, the stage was set for a serious confrontation.

How would you solve this standoff?

A wise man in Musa's court perceived the impending disaster and suggested that the Mansa kiss the ground in front of the Sultan's throne in praise of Allah, the creator of all things. The Mansa was quite pleased with this suggestion and proceeded to kiss the ground in front of the sultan's throne, saying a silent prayer to Allah. The sultan then stood up and invited the emperor of Mali to come and sit on the throne beside him.

Before leaving Cairo, Mansa recruited many gifted professionals to return with him to Mali to enhance their educational structures and support intellectual, religious, and artistic growth.

As they neared Mecca and the caravan was preparing to make its grand entrance, the Mansa was amazed to encounter so many travelers from countries he had never even heard of.

For the twelve days of his pilgrimage, Mansa Musa wore a plain, seamless white garment, identical to that worn by every other worshiper, regardless of his status. All worshipers in Mecca were equal before God. Therefore, Mansa Musa became merely a worshiper among many other worshipers.

The Return Journey to Mali.
SORRY SIR, WE DON'T HAVE ENOUGH GOLD TO MAKE IT BACK HOME.

As they prepared for the return to Mali, it was the unpleasant duty of Chief Stewart to inform the Mansa that there wasn't enough gold left in the treasury to purchase the supplies needed for the return journey. The Mansa had to borrow large sums of gold from wealthy Egyptian merchants at exorbitant interest rates. He repaid these loans as soon as he returned home, further increasing Cairo's inflation.

Student loans?

Mansa Musa believed that scholarship and education in his provinces were critically important to the continued success of the Empire. To advance these objectives, he provided royal patronage to support the work of the nation's leading scholars and financial assistance to the nation's best and brightest students.

The Mansa built universities, libraries, and mosques throughout the empire.

The magnificent library at Timbuktu was said to rival the famous Library of Alexandria in terms of the number and variety of manuscripts.

Achievements:

1. Mansa Musa was a great general who never lost a battle.
2. It is said that he freed one slave each and every day of his rule.
3. In Timbuktu, Musa used his wealth to build schools, universities, libraries, and mosques.
4. He was known to be a wise, effective, and compassionate ruler.
5. Mansa was a deeply devout man, adhering faithfully to the principles of Islam.
6. His support of scholarship and education was legendary.

Mansa Musa died in 1337 at the age of 57. The empire was inherited by his sons, who could not hold the empire together. They were unable to fend off civil wars and the numerous invading armies, including Europeans. Just two generations after Mansa Musa's death, his world record net worth was gone.

CHAPTER TEN

Out of Africa Came Eve

I want to introduce you to a quiet storm. This storm is in the form of a little lady. She was Black, barely four feet tall, and weighed 60 lbs. She caused a firestorm of controversy that shook the anthropological and evolutionary world to their very core. She called into question the long-held theory that man evolved from apes.

The lady has a very simple, common name. Can you guess her name, or where she came from?

Her name is Lucy, from the Beatles song "Lucy in the Sky with Diamonds." Her remains were found at Hadar, Ethiopia on November 24, 1974, by a team of anthropologists led by Donald Johnson. Lucy's remains were unlike any previous human remains that the researchers had ever seen. The numerous things that identified this discovery as one of the most significant finds in human history stirred their excitement.

1. The most remarkable thing about Lucy is that she is 3.2 million years old.

2. As indicated above, she was less than 4ft tall and weighed just 60lbs.
3. She walked upright just like you and me, but she was also adept at climbing trees.
4. Her teeth were just like yours and mine, no canine teeth like chimps.
5. Her brain was smaller than ours (approximately the size of a grapefruit).
6. She was a social being and lived in a small family community.

The researchers found an astounding number of her remains: pelvis, arms, ribs, leg, teeth, and portions of the skull. Totalled, the pieces amounted to about 40% of what appeared to be a three million-year old Hominid skeleton (Hominid simply means ancient Human).

After extensive analysis and evaluation, the research team came to the conclusion that what they had just discovered was a brand new human species, a new human ancestor, born in Africa. She was older and unlike any other hominid species previously unearthed.

Before the excavation at Hadar was terminated in 1974, the team collected additional skeletal remains belonging to several hundred different individuals who lived in Lucy's community. State-of-the-art dating confirmed that they were her contemporaries.

As the TV ad goes, "But wait there's more"

As if finding Lucy were not enough, in 1991, anthropologists discovered another bombshell. Lucy, it seems had a sister, who was 1.2 million years older than she. In the Afar Desert in Ethiopia in 1991, Scientist discovered a large collection of skeletal remains belonging to another ancient female. They determined that she was an even earlier human ancestor. She was given the nickname Ardi. Her superior age placed Ardi at the top of the list of ancient human ancestors.

State-of-the-art scientific dating placed Ardi's age at 4.4 million years. Before completing their work at Afar, the team excavated an astounding 125 pieces of Ardi's remains. These remains included her skull, teeth, arms, hands, legs, pelvis, and feet.

While Ardi was taller than her sister at 4.7 feet, she was not as heavy, weighing only 50 lbs. But, also like her sister and like us, she walked upright, and she, too, was adept at climbing trees. Her brain size was also smaller than ours.

The awesome discovery of Lucy and Ardi shattered the long-held belief of Darwinists and evolutionists that humans evolved from chimpanzees. To date, no one has found ancient remains of chimps that are older than 4.4 million years.

Today, you can see Lucy's remains in museums. The discovery of Lucy's remains is now recognized worldwide as the most famous discovery of an ancient human ancestor ever made. She was the first hominid to really capture the public's attention and imagination. Hundreds of thousands of people from around the world flock to museums to view the original or replicas of Lucy's remains.

What do you think was the reaction of European and American scientists to the discovery of Lucy and Ardi?

The publication of these momentous discoveries in Ethiopia was met with a torrent of scientific papers and seminars attempting to refute or call into question the conclusions of the Hadar and Afar anthropologists. Nonetheless, the evidence remained irrefutable and today the fruit of the digs in Ethiopia is universally accepted as scientific truth. Thus, the international scientific community has come kicking and scratching to the unavoidable conclusion that Africa is the cradle of humanity, as confirmed in anthropological studies, DNA studies, and the Bible..

CHAPTER ELEVEN

The Mother of us all, Mitochondria Eve

What would you say if I told you that everyone, repeat *everyone*, living today shares an African ancestor who lived 200,000 years ago?

In 1987, researchers Rebecca Cann, Mark Stoneking, and Allan C. Wilson, working out of Berkeley University, published an article in Nature Magazine that was nothing short of a scientific bombshell. It called into serious question existing theories of human evolution. The researchers compiled solid evidence establishing that every person on Earth today can trace their lineage back to a single maternal ancestor who lived about 200,000 years ago in Africa.

The team collected mitochondrial DNA from 147 individuals living in four different geographic locations: Africa, Asia, Australia, and Europe.

Before we continue we need to define some of our terms.

What part of every human cell is large and in charge?

THE NUCLEUS

The nucleus of a cell is the executive headquarters, or the command center, of each and every cell in the body. It controls all of the functions and activities of the cell.

DNA

The most important part of the nucleus is its DNA. It controls and directs everything that happens in the cell. It is the main computer of the nucleus, directing the activities of each cell with respect to growth, repair, and reproduction. The functions of every cell are defined, directed, and controlled by the DNA. DNA also determines the destiny of the cell, whether it will become a heart, muscle, eye, kidney, skin, hair, or brain cell. Finally, it determines when it's time for a cell to pack it in and cease to be.

Our DNA is inherited from all of our ancestors. Individually, we get half of our DNA from our mothers and half from our fathers. The DNA that an individual receives from his parents is distinct from the DNA of all other humans, past or present. No two individuals share the same DNA, except identical twins.

MITOCHONDRIA

Mitochondria (mtDNA) is a component of a cell that is not located in the nucleus. It is the energy powerhouse of the cell and converts the food we eat into the energy that the body needs. The most defining feature of mitochondrial DNA (and what we will focus on today) is that it is only passed on to the next generation by the female. This transmission occurs without change, mix, or alteration during the sexual union.

Exactly what the mother receives from her mother, is what she transmits to her daughters. Male children do receive mtDNA from their mothers as well, but it is never transmitted during the reproduction process. When sperm attaches itself to the egg in reproduction, the egg cell strips the sperm of its mtDNA.

As mentioned at the top of this presentation, researchers using mtDNA have determined that every person on Earth today can trace their maternal ancestry back to a Black woman who lived in Africa 200,000 years ago. Scientists have labeled this maternal ancestor

"Mitochondria Eve" and described her as a dark haired, dark skinned woman from continental Africa.

Notwithstanding the implication of the name, the scientists recognized that Mitochondria Eve was not the only or first woman on earth during her lifetime. There were many women who lived before and after Eve. Yet for some unexplained reason, it was Mitochondria Eve's mtDNA that got passed down unchanged through generations of female offspring. All women alive today will continue to pass Eve's mtDNA down to their female offspring indefinitely.

Scientists continue to debate and explore just what was so special about this woman that allowed only her mtDNA to be transmitted down through 200,000 years of females.

MtDNA can be used to track your ancestral tree as far back as hundreds of generations. That is what makes ancestry search services such as Ancestry.com and 23 and Me so popular. MtDNA has also been used to help forensic scientists make identifications when tissue remains are too damaged or degraded to obtain useable DNA.

The facts of this presentation represent a powerful affirmation of how few and insignificant the differences are among humans today. Through Mitochondria Eve, we are all related and comprise one family of man.

THE WASHITAW NATION

The Washitaw nation is one of several black American tribes that were in the continental US before Columbus, before the birth of Christ and thousands of years before the Native Americans.

This Bird Mounds complex is the Washitaw nation's most sacred site.
Archeologist place it's date of origin at 2000 BC.

ANCIENT BLACK EGYPTIANS IN THE UNITED STATES GRAND CANYON

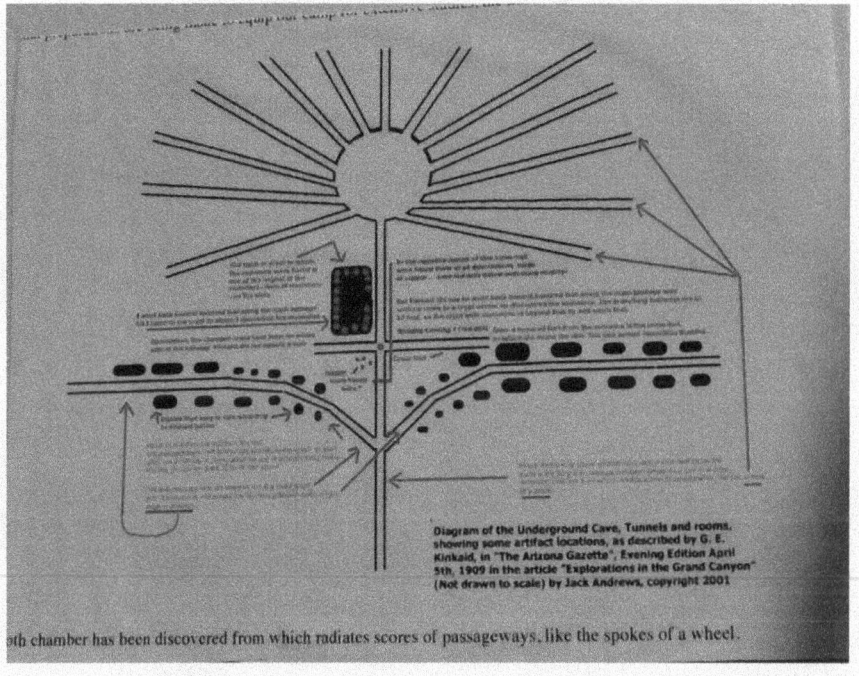

A sketch of the massive underground tunnel built by the Egyptians In the Grand Canyon around the year 1700BC. This massive tunnel could Accommodate up to 1,000 residents.

A room filled with mummies of tall Africans found in the tunnel network complex built by ancient Egyptians in the Grand Canyon.

Artifacts from the massive underground cave found in the Grand Canyon, on display at the Smithsonian Institute.

An Egyptian Pharaoh with apparent oriental eyes.

Kon San Bushman of the Kalahari, Southern Africa

*The Bushmen of the Kalahari have what we recognize as oriental eyes.
However, they have had those oriental eyes for thousands of years before the emergence of the Chinese.*

Grandmother and granddaughter of the Kon San people (bushmen of the Kalahari).

CAHOKIA, THE ANCIENT MYSTERY CITY IN MIDDLE AMERICA

This ancient African cosmopolitan city, built in Middle America flourished around 1050 AD. It was the largest commercial center in America at that time. It was located under the present day St Louis, Missouri. Anthropologist were amazed to discover that this city was built by skilled Urban planners.

This pyramid was the centerpiece of the City of Cahokia as shown in the layout above. It is the oldest archeological site in the continental US. This pyramid could only have been built by Africans, because Africans were the only ancient people at that time with the know-how to build pyramids.

PREHISTORIC AFRICANS SOUTH OF THE BORDER

21 of these finely sculptured African heads were unearthed in Central Mexico around 1500 BC. They represent an ancient Civilization called the Olmec. The average weight was between 10 and 40 tons, the height 9 to 10 feet and the average 2000years

On the back of one of these giant heads was found African style cornrows, confirming its identity as African.

This pyramid is located at La Venta, the capital city of the Olmec world.

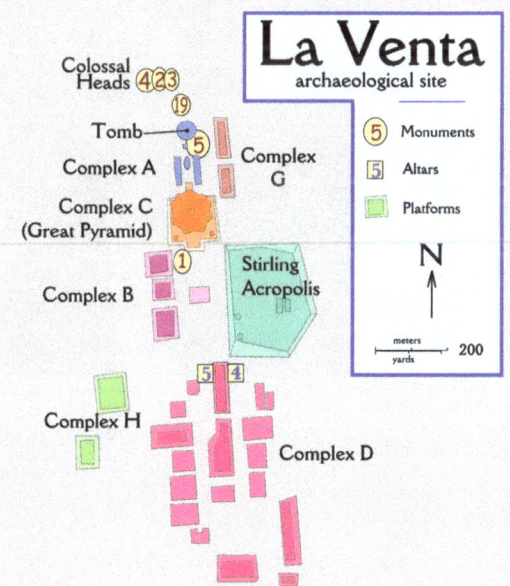

The layout of the Olmec capital city of La Venta. Complex C in the middle is the great pyramid. At the top are three colossal African heads looking to the east from wince they came.

In addition to the giant colossal heads, the Olmec also sculptured smaller figurines with unmistakable African features

THE ANCIENT BLACK EGYPTIANS

This was the first Egyptian pharaoh. He came to the throne in 3168 BC

Anenhotep II 18th dynasty 1390 - 1353

Clearly, a royal Brother

This incense burner is from the oldest civilization in the world, the Nubian civilization of Tar-Seti which flourished some 6,000 years before the emergence of the mighty Egyptian civilization.

The Ancient Sahara Lakes

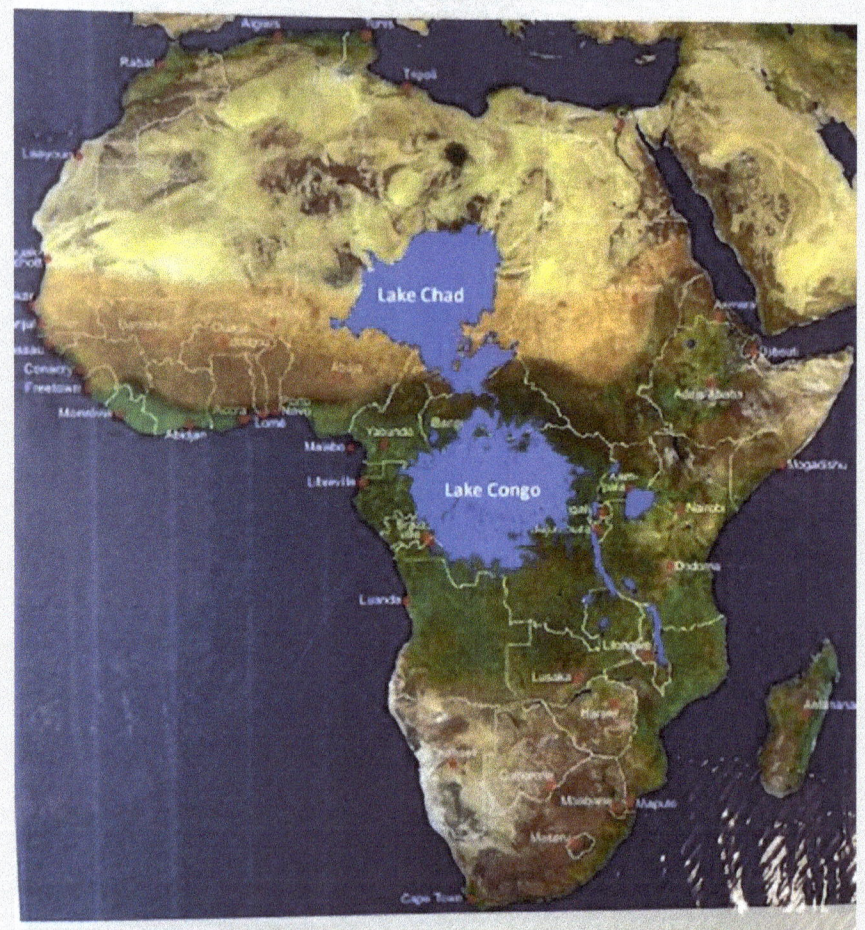

The Egyptians built large ships to convey people and merchandise up and down the Nile river. The Nile is the longest river in the world. They also built large ships to navigate the enormous lakes in the Sahara, before it dried up.

GREEK PHILOSOPHY IS ACTUALLY STOLEN EGYPTIAN PHILOSOPHY

Professor James' ground breaking book established beyond question or doubt where Greek philosophy originated, and it is believed that it cost him his life

THE GOLDEN EMPIRE OF MALI, AND THE RICHEST RULING BROTHERS IN THE WORLD

Mansa (king) Abubakari of Mali was the king who gave up power and wealth to peruse a dream of discovery.

Mansa Abubakari sailed toward the Americas with 2,000 ships and landed somewhere in Brazil.

Mansa (king) Musa, Abubakari's brother was an enlightened monarch who was also the richest man in the world in 1300 AD.

Mansa Musa made the Hajj to Mecca with a caravan of 60,000.

AFRICANS ESTABLISHED THE FIRST TWO GREAT CIVILIZATIONS IN CHINA: THE XIA, AND THE SHANG CIVILIZATIONS.

Notice the African head in the middle of this bronze masterpiece.

The above sculpture and the one below, are from the Shang civilization.

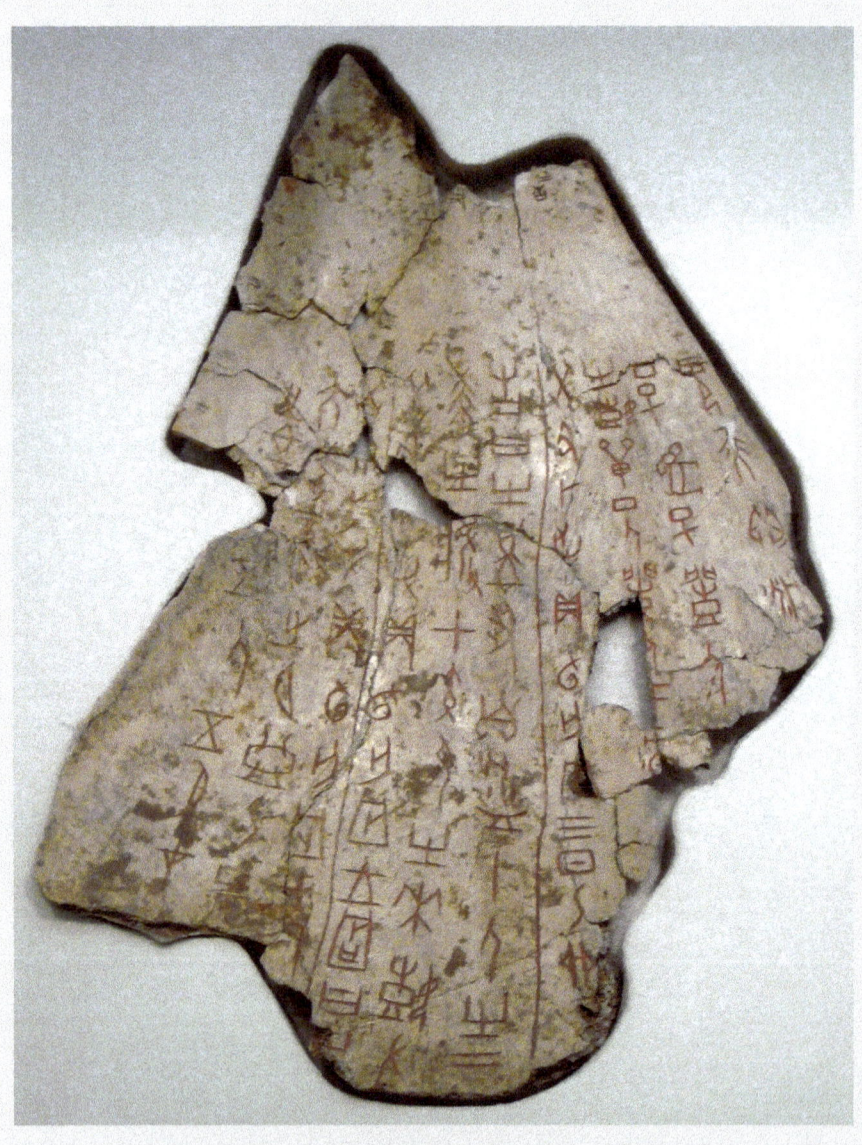

The Shang used the shells of large Turtles, stones and the scapula (shoulder blade) of Oxen to write script. As a result, there is an enormous amount of documentation of the life and contribution of this great African civilization.

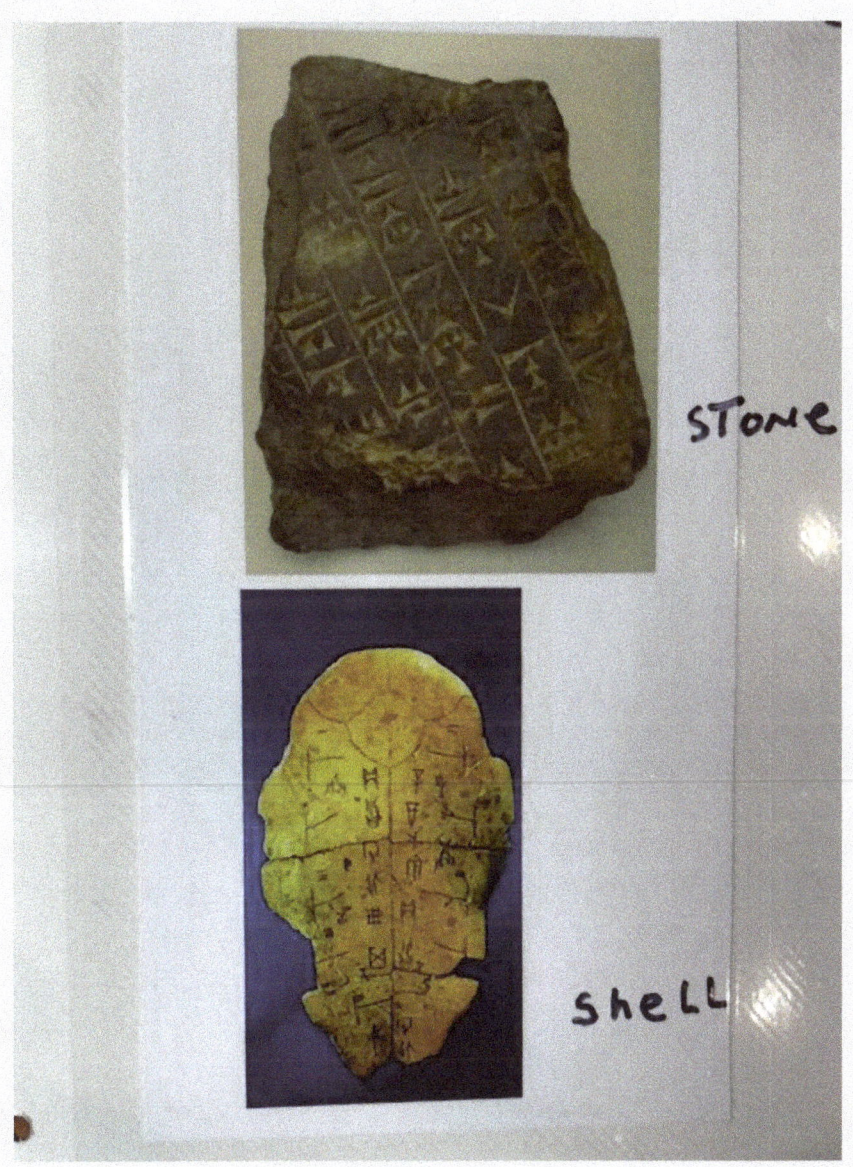

stone

shell

LUCY, OUR ANCIENT SISTER

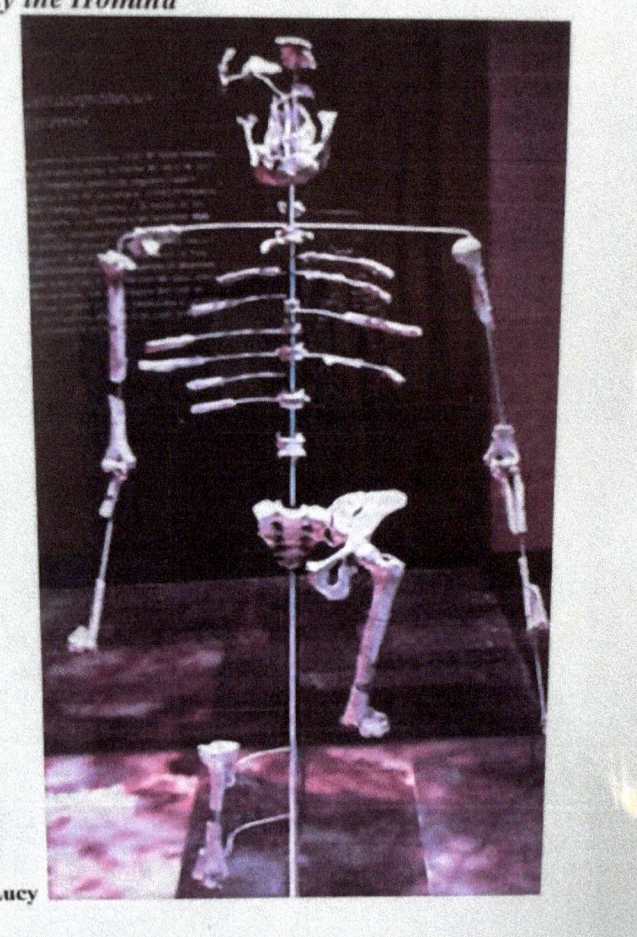

Lucy the Homind

Lucy

This little lady is Lucy. She is 4ft tall, weighs 50 lb., walks upright and has teeth like ours, not canine like Chimps. She was found in Ethiopia in 1974. Carbon dating placed her age at 3.2 million years.

THE BLACK MADONNAS

The Black Virgin of Monserrat, Spain. This is how she looks today

This is how she looked in 1961 when I saw her in Barcelona. There are over 500 Black Madonnas in Europe today. All are held in the highest esteem by local worshipers. There has never been a movement by the Church to remove them, or to challenge their authenticity.

A Black Madonna and child in England today

The Black Madonna at Chartres, France

A Black Madonna and child in France. There are over 300 such Madonnas in France today.

The famous Black Madonna of Czestochwa, Poland. It is widely reported and believed that this Madonna was painted by one of the Gospel writers. Who? St. Luke.

Note that the Popes are worshiping a Black Madonna and Child situated on a high alter. This chapel is located in the Vatican. Only the highest level of clergy have access to this sacred chapel. Apparently the Popes see no conflict of conscious worshiping a white Madonna in public, and a black Madonna in secret.

Newsweek scientists finally acknowledge what we have known all along, that Adam and Eve were Black. The magazine is belatedly acknowledging what scientists have known for centuries, that the first people to walk the earth were black Africans. I didn't know the ancestors wore Jerry curl hair!

Conquered Israelites being carried away by the Assyrian army in 732 BC. This image strongly suggests that the Israelites were people of color. That sure looks like "happy to be nappy" hair to me.

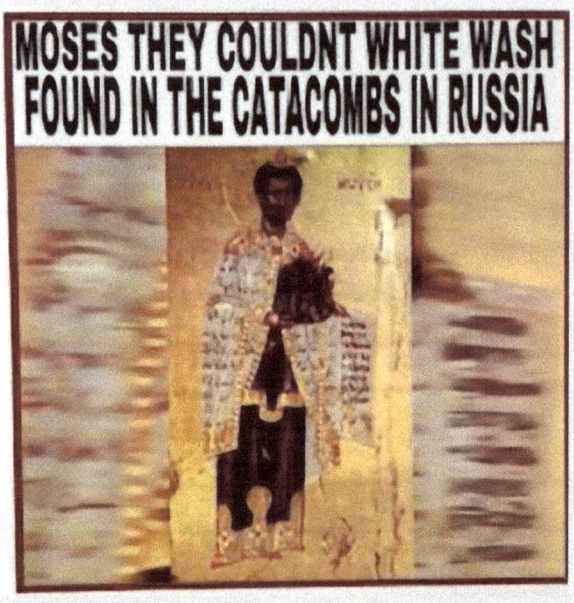

An image of a Black Moses found in the Russian Catacombs (underground burial cave)

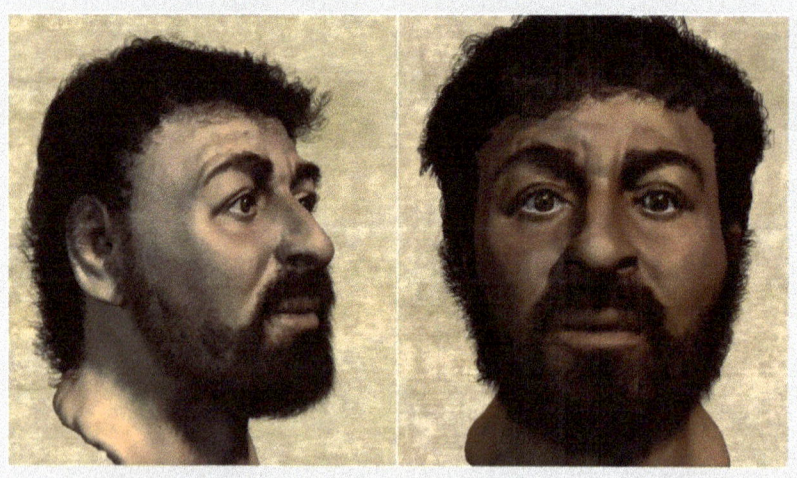

A computerized image of a man who lived at the same time as Jesus and in the same location.
The project Leader, Dr. Neaves acknowledged that while the facial features and structure are scientifically accurate, the color of the skin and texture of the hair are less so.

Leonardo Da Vinci's painting of Jesus as commissioned by Pope Alexander VI. The Pope insisted that Da Vinci use his illegitimate and immoral son, Caesar as the model. The Pope was determined to rid the Church of all images of a black and brown Jesus. Da Vinci labeled the painting, "Salvador Mundi" or "Savior of the World."

*Warner Sallman's "Head of Christ," the most reproduced and circulated image of Jesus ever. It was reproduced over 700,000 times and came to define what Jesus looked like for millions of individuals and generations of believers. For countless devout Christian, it **is** the image of the son of God. In reality it was simply the rendering of a 1940 commercial artist. Since no image of Jesus was produced during his lifetime, all subsequent images of Him, past and present are the product of imagination of the artist who produced them. If this is Jesus, what happened to the black child in the arms of the Black Madonnas.*

The earliest known image of Christ – in the Coptic Museum in Cairo, Egypt. This painting is older than the image of the black Christ in a church of Rome dated 530 AD.

Part Three

THE BIBLE IS THE BLACK MAN'S HISTORY

CHAPTER TWELVE

The Bible is the Black Man's History #1

Let's get started with a question to get your brains warmed up. In what language were the Ten Commandments written? Hint: it wasn't Hebrew. The answer will be given at the end of the chapter.

Today, I'm going to take you on a journey into Biblical truths that you may not be aware of. Much of what you have read, heard, and seen in TV, print, and movies about the great people of the Bible is a lie. Today, with God's help, we're going to put the spotlight on something some regard as an uncomfortable truth about our Bible.

In one of his last speeches, Dr. Martin Luther King Jr. said, "No lie can live forever; truth thrust to the ground will rise again."

What have white influential religious leaders over the centuries been saying about the presence of Black folks in the Bible?
Since 1505, white Christian leadership, supported by Popes, theologians, and political leaders has characterized all important biblical personalities as Caucasian.

Hollywood told us that if we want to know what Moses of the Bible looked like, just check out Charleston Heston in the movie *The*

Ten Commandments. Similarly, if we want to know what the Egyptian queen Cleopatra looked like, just have a look at Elizabeth Taylor in the film *Cleopatra*.

Television documentaries from CBS, NBC, ABC, and CNN, especially those aired during holiday seasons, would have us believe that all of the beloved personalities in the Bible were Caucasian.

White historians and authors have whitewashed entire black nations, peoples, and empires that are so much a part of the Bible story: the Egyptians, Babylonians, Philistines, Canaanites, and Samaritans—all were black nations at the time of the Old Testament.

The assumption is simple. White theologians and white church leaders want everyone to believe the big lie that black folks did not contribute anything significant to the Biblical story.

Now that we have dealt with some fiction, let's explore some truths.

Have you ever given any serious thought to the origin, identity, and role that Black people may have played in the biblical story? Most of us have not. Today, it is becoming more and more evident that scripture, science, and history support that dark-skinned people were prominent throughout the entire Bible, especially in the Old Testament. One biblical researcher concluded that 95% of all activities in the Old Testament occurred on the continent of Africa.

The Garden of Eden

Let's start by directing our journey into the Bible as the Black man's history with a look at where it all started, the Garden of Eden.

Where does the Bible suggest that the Garden of Eden was located?
To answer that question, let's first go to Gen. 2:10-14. All four of the rivers mentioned in this passage of scripture are located in Africa. Therefore, the logical conclusion is that the Garden of Eden was

planted by God on the fertile continent of Africa. Today, there is a consensus among archaeologists that the Garden of Eden probably flourished somewhere in the country of Ethiopia. There is good reason for this belief: the oldest excavated human skeletal remains in the world were unearthed in Ethiopia.

Today's historians, for the most part, reluctantly accept irrefutable archaeological and anthropological evidence that modern man first made his appearance on the Earth in Africa some 200,000 years ago. This early ancestor was not related to apes or chimps but were anatomically and intellectually similar to human beings today. It is important to note that 200,000 years ago, the Black race was the only race on the planet.

Is there any DNA evidence to corroborate the above anthropological findings?

Recently, three teams of scientists from different locations around the world conducted separate DNA studies to ascertain the origin of humankind. They collected hundreds of DNA specimens from people in nations all around the globe. While the methods and parameters of each study were different, the findings were consistent with the anthropological conclusion that the human race, as we know it today, first emerged in Africa some 200,000 years ago.

Adam and Eve

Given what we have learned, can we make any definitive statements about Adam and Eve? While we do not know exactly what Adam and Eve looked like, we can be assured that they did not look like the images we have all seen of a naked white couple in a shy intimate embrace in the middle of a lovely garden. This image is at variance with the above conclusions that (1) the first humans on earth appeared in Africa some 200,000 years ago, (2) the Bible tells us that the Garden of Eden was located in Africa, and (3) there were no white people on the earth 200,000 years ago.

Is it possible for white couples to produce black offspring?
According to Western history revisionists, Noah had one black son, his youngest, Ham. A good question to ask at this point is how Noah and Mrs. Noah produced this one black child when, according to these same revisionists, the other sons were white. Today's scientists, in a rare demonstration of unanimity, agree that black couples can and often do produce fair or white offspring. However, **they are equally persuaded that it is genetically impossible for white couples to produce dark-skinned offspring.** Therefore Noah, Mrs. Noah, or both would have had to have been black to produce this one black child.

Can we apply the above principle to Adam and Eve? Following the scientific data to its logical conclusion, if Adam and Eve were white, they would only be able to produce white offspring. Then the question to be asked is where did the black folks come from?

Long Overdue Confessions

Two white magazines with international circulations are having an awakening regarding the true origin of humankind. Respected scientists and anthropologists writing in Newsweek and National Geographic magazines concluded that Adam and Eve were indeed Africans. This turn-around is certainly a confirmation of Dr. King's admonition that "no lie can live forever; truth thrust to the ground will rise again." The image of a black Adam and Eve is displayed on the front cover of the January 11, 1988, issue of Newsweek. Look it up!

In summary, there can be little doubt, especially when confronted with indisputable anthropological, DNA, and journalistic evidence that the first human couple to appear on the Earth was African and that the lovely Garden that God created for them was located in the motherland. This evidence more than satisfies the biblical criteria of "two witnesses."

Egypt and the Old Testament

The country of Egypt is mentioned in 588 verses and 32 books of the Bible. These numbers speak of the importance of Egypt in the Biblical narrative.

The constant mentioning throughout the Old Testament gives rise to an important question: just who were these Egyptians, and why were they such a vital part of God's Holy word.

In 1974, a UN conference hosted in Cairo, Egypt was held to determine once and for all just who the ancient Egyptians were. Of the 20 international scholars in attendance (including Egyptologists from Egypt), only two were Black: Dr. Cheik Anta Diop, the brilliant scholar from Senegal, and Dr. Theophile Obenga, the noted scholar from the Congo. At the conclusion of the conference and following rigorous debate, all of the other 18 scholars agreed with the argument put forth by the two Black scholars that the ancient Egyptians who built the Pyramids with great precision, a splendid prehistoric civilization, and erected the massive statue of the Sphinx, were indeed Black Africans. The only delegation that raised objections to the conclusion that the Ancient Egyptians were black Africans was the Egyptian delegation. Therefore, when you see the words Egyptian and Egypt in the Bible, think African and African nation.

The Egyptian civilization that lasted for over 3,000 years included the period of the Old Testament.

Noah, the Ark Builder

Now let's talk about Noah, the Ark builder. Noah built his Ark in the desert some nine generations after the death of Adam. Earlier, we established that our first ancestors, Adam and Eve, were Africans. Could Noah and his family, nine generations from Adam, be anything other than Africans? Further, if there were white people on earth during Noah's life time, a good question would be, where did they come from?

A bit of trivia. Who was Noah's grandaddy? Methuselah.

How did white racists in Western society distort Noah's story?

Over time, certain Western religious, political, and pro-slavery groups began to spread the following false doctrines:

1. Because Ham was cursed by Noah, his skin became black, totally disregarding the fact that Ham was not cursed by his father. Further, there is no evidence in the Bible that records Ham having a change of color. Neither are there any instances in scripture where God turned someone's skin black as a punishment. Quite to the contrary. See Numbers 12:10, where God turned Moses' sister, Miriam, white for rebelling against her brother's authority.
2. Western racists also claimed that, due to Noah's curse, Ham and his descendants were predestined to be the servants of his brothers. None of this happened, yet this false teaching was used by Europeans and Americans to justify racism and the inhumane enslavement of people of color.

How did Ham become the personification of blackness to the Western world?

As the story of the post-flood family began to filter through the centuries and was interpreted by various Islamic, Christian, and Jewish scholars, Noah's son Ham became the personification of blackness and servitude. In reality, Ham's dark skin was not the result of a curse by his father. He and his brothers were blessed with dark skin at birth some 95 years before the flood. His descendants not only did not serve their brothers but were the creators of the two greatest civilizations of the ancient world: the Egyptian and the Babylon civilizations. In addition, they created many other great civilizations on the continent of Africa and around the world prior to the invasion of the Europeans.

Noah's curse

Gen 9:20-22,24-27: "Noah, a man of the soil, proceeded to plant a vineyard. When he drank some of its wine, he became drunk and lay uncovered inside his tent. Ham, the father of Canaan, saw his father's nakedness and told his two brothers outside."

24-27: "When he awoke from his wine and found out what his youngest son had done to him, Noah said, "Cursed be Canaan! The lowest of slaves will he be to his brothers" (NIV). In biblical times, there were no such terms as grandfather or grandson. Ham was Noah's youngest son, but Noah placed the curse on Ham's youngest son Canaan, or, as we would say today, on his grandson. The youngest male child in the entire family was traditionally called the "the youngest son." Why did Noah curse his grandson, Canaan?

Let's have a closer look at some puzzling facts about the Noah story. Noah's curse was not directed towards any particular race. Scripture does not record any instances where God ever pronounced a curse on Black people. The truth of the matter is that it is highly unlikely that God would ever honor the curse of a man freshly awakening from a drunken stupor. Prov. 26:2: "Like a fluttering sparrow or a darting swallow, an undeserved curse will not land on its intended victim."

Let's do a little Law and Order CSI investigation. When I read of Noah's curse, several interesting thoughts came to mind:

1. How did Noah know what was done to him? This implies that something unpleasant was done to him in his drunken state that he was aware of but was unable to resist.

2. The fact that Noah placed the curse on Canaan implies a possible visitation by Canaan that involved more than just a look at his nakedness.
3. Noah expressed no interest in, nor knowledge of, Ham seeing him naked.
4. Nakedness is not usually associated with drunkenness, otherwise bars and taverns would be filled with naked patrons. So, something else must have been going on here.

In the bible, God instructs Noah's descendants to increase and fill the Earth. Gen 9: "Then God blessed Noah and his sons, saying to them be fruitful and increase in number and fill the Earth." Therefore, in obedience to God, Noah's offspring populated the entire post-flood world with black and brown offspring

The Sons of Noah

Shem's descendants are associated with the ancient countries located in what we now call the Middle East. Shem is a direct ancestor of Abraham, the father of the Hebrew lineage which includes the bloodline of Jesus Christ. The world's three great religions sprang from Shem's descendants: Judaism, Christianity and Islam.

Noah's "forgotten" son is Japheth. The Bible makes minimal mention of Japheth or his offspring. Japheth's descendants originally migrated into the Caucasus region of Eastern Europe, which is now a part of Russia. Japheth is celebrated in the Western world as "the father of the Caucasian race." His descendants were originally people of color, as were his brothers.

Ham, the father of mighty nations

The sons of Ham, for the most part, settled in North Africa and created great nations and mighty kingdoms. Other members of the clan migrated to more distant parts of the world.

There is no question but that the achievements of Ham's offspring down through the ages far exceeded the accomplishments of the offspring of his brothers. In addition, there is considerably more written in the Bible about the descendants of Ham, their land, and people than his brother's offspring. So much for the misplaced curse.

Canaan

Canaan was Ham's youngest son, the one cursed by his tipsy grandfather for mysterious reasons. Canaan's descendants settled in the Holy Land region: Palestine, Lebanon, and Jordan. The land of Palestine, formerly called Canaan, is the land promised by God to the Israelites. Today, Palestine is occupied by the modern state of Israel.

Why was the Canaan called the land loved and hated by God?

The land of Canaan, which was established by the descendants of Canaan, was considered prime real estate by God, who labeled it "the land of milk and honey." It was so prized by God that he allowed his son and our savior to be born in the land of Canaan. Yes, the town of Bethlehem is located in Canaan, which is located in northeast Africa. God's anger toward the indigenous people of Canaan was due to their decadent behavior and worship of many other Gods. It had nothing to do with the color of their skin or a curse.

Hebrew, the language of the Israelites, is actually an African language. It originated from a large family of African languages known as "Afroasiatic." Hebrew was not reduced to written script until 320 years after the giving of the Ten Commandments. Hebrew was the language spoken in the land of Canaan for over a thousand years before the arrival of Abraham, Isaac, Jacob and their descendants. As a result, the Israelites soon abandoned whatever language they were speaking at the time and adopted the Hebrew speech of the Canaanites.

Notwithstanding the above, after being in Egypt for 430 years, it would seem logical to conclude that all of the Israelite slaves spoke Egyptian as their primary language. This would include any learned men among them. There is no evidence to suggest that the Israelite slaves in Egypt at that time could read, write, or speak anything another than Egyptian..

CHAPTER THIRTEEN

The Bible is the Black Man's History #2.

Nimrod, the first great post-flood king and empire builder

If you check with Mr. Google or search Bible Dictionaries, you will find an abundance of information about the mighty ruler Nimrod, his life, accomplishments, and everything else your inquiring mind would want to know about this extraordinary man—except the fact that he was Black.

Nimrod was a giant of a man who walked the earth only two generations after the global flood. His grandfather, Ham, was one of the eight people who rode out the massive flood in Noah's ark. Ham's son, Cush, was Nimrod's Dad. (The very name Cush means black.) In Gen. 8:9, the Bible calls Nimrod a "mighty hunter" because of his legendary skill. However, when he matured, in addition to becoming a mighty warrior, Nimrod would prove to be an extraordinarily effective political leader.

Very few students of the Bible today realize that the first post-flood kingdom mentioned in Scripture was under the leadership of a remarkable Black man the likes of which the world had never seen before. Nimrod became the world's first empire-builder. Under his leadership, all of the people of the post-flood world were united as one (Gen. 11:6).

How many languages were spoken when Nimrod came to power?
Everyone born after the flood was a descendant of the eight survivors. They spoke the same language and lived in the same geographic location. As their numbers increased, they began to search for a more expanded location to settle. They settled in the rich, fertile plains of Shinar in Iraq. Through conquests and negotiations, Nimrod soon emerged as the most powerful man on Earth.

In the plains of Shinar, Noah's black great-grandchildren, under the leadership of Nimrod, developed stone working and brick masonry skills and set about building durable edifices and cities. They were determined to build structures sturdy enough to withstand the ravages of another massive flood. Apparently, the devastating impact of the flood was securely imprinted on their minds. The reason God sent the flood in the first place seemed to occupy a more obscure place in their conscious awareness.

Prior to Nimrod, the world had never witnessed the construction of a multi-state empire. The book of Genesis records that Nimrod planned and oversaw the development and expansion of many cities, including the city of Babel and Babylon. (Babylon today would be located in the country of Iraq.) Gen 10:10: "The first centers of his kingdom were Babylon, Erech, Akkad and Calneh…" How often do you think the people of Iraq today celebrate Nimrod as their first great empire builder? Unfortunately, they never did and probably never will.

Thus, the entire post-flood world was under the authority of this extraordinary black leader. God himself acknowledged that unless he put a stop to this man's power and ambition, his aspirations would appear to be unlimited. "The Lord said, 'if as one people speaking the same language they have begun to do this, then nothing they plan to do will be impossible for them" (Gen. 11:6, NIV).

Why did Nimrod want to build a tower at Babel?
At Babel, Nimrod's administration decided to make a name for itself by launching the greatest construction project the world had ever seen: nothing less than a tower that would reach into the heavens. This would ensure their survival in the event of another global flood. The foundation of the tower was massive and would have overshadowed the foundation of any of Egypt's great pyramids, including its largest at Giza, which is reputed to have the largest foundation of any man-made structure in the world today.

Was Nimrod the Great guilty of any sin?
To be sure he was. Bolstered by his inflated sense of pride and his administrative and military successes, Nimrod saw no reason to share his power with God. Therefore, he had turned away from the God of his ancestors. God witnessed the building of the tower and, knowing its purpose and intent, became angry. "Let us go down and confound their language, that they may not understand one another's speech" (Gen 11:5-9).

God afflicted the tower workers with multiple languages, making work and communication impossible. As a result, work on the project halted and was soon abandoned. That is how the Tower of Babel got its name. God grouped those speaking the same language and dispersed them around the globe to establish tribes and clans. "So, the Lord scattered them abroad from there over the face of all the Earth" (Gen11:8).

Moses

From a previous discussion, we learned that whenever we see the terms *Egyptian* or *Egypt* in the Bible, we are to think *African* or *African nation*.

You are all familiar with this story. Around the time of Moses' birth, the king of Egypt issued an edict calling for the death of all male Hebrew newborn babies.

This edict was issued because the pharaoh, witnessing the explosive growth of the Hebrew slave population, became fearful that they might become numerous enough to lay siege to and take over his government.

Jochebed, a Hebrew woman of the line of Levi, gave birth to a male child. His father was a black Hebrew descendant of Shem, as were Abraham, Isaac, and Jacob. The baby's skin color was probably that of his ancestors. Worried that her son might be killed, Jochebed hid him for three months. Exodus 2:3: "When she could hide him no longer, she got a papyrus basket for him and coated it with tar and pitch. Then she placed the child in it and put it among the reeds along the bank of the Nile."

Did the pharaoh's daughter know that baby she found was a Hebrew child and, if so, how?

Pharaoh's daughter immediately identified this abandoned infant as Hebrew because he was circumcised. "This is one of the Hebrews' children" (Ex 2:6). Even to this day, Jewish male infants are circumcised eight days after birth. The princess felt compassion and love for this child and determined in her heart to adopt him and raise him in the palace as her son.

According to Jewish historian Josephus, the princess told her father, the pharaoh, how she discovered the babe and said that she thought it proper to adopt him for her son and that Pharaoh should accept the child as heir to his throne. "She put the child in her father's arms and he hugged him." Would the most powerful black monarch in the world accept a child as his grandson and heir if that child did not look like him and his people?

Act 7:22—Moses was accorded the most exquisite education available anywhere in the ancient world. The Egypt of that time had no equal in quality of their institutions of higher learning. Scholars from all over the world traveled to Egypt to avail themselves of the wisdom and knowledge of learned Black masters.

Party time at the palace; let the good times roll!
While a young man in the palace of the most powerful country in the world, Moses took advantage of the palatial pleasures and privileges afforded a grandson and heir to the pharaoh. There is an area of the palace referred to in scriptures as the "tabernacle, or tent of Ham" (Ps. 78:51). This Tent of Ham was known to house a harem of the most beautiful women in all of Africa. Moses, like any other young man, found the allure of such an enticing playground irresistible.

Responding to God's call
Shortly after this period in Moses' life, God determined it was time to call Moses to begin to put into motion his plan for the destiny of his chosen people. Moses' heart began to change. He no longer coveted the privileges of royalty. As God's plan began to unfold in his life, Moses became more and more uncomfortable with being called the son of Pharaoh's daughter. Instead, he felt the urge to connect with the heritage of his Hebrew parents and ancestors.

An interesting speculation: had Moses chosen not to accept God's call on his life and continued to enjoy the power and pleasures of the palace, he would have been Pharaoh when God demanded of the Egyptian Pharaoh to "Let my people go." It's interesting to speculate just how Moses as pharaoh would have responded to that historic encounter.

Moses became a wanted man after killing an Egyptian who was abusing a Hebrew brother. Now a fugitive on the lamb, Moses thought it wise to take flight from Egypt. Unbeknownst to him, this was all part of God's plan to prepare him for the demanding challenges that lay ahead.

A little background history before we get to the Exodus.
When Jacob's son, Joseph, became the second-in-command in Egypt during a seven-year famine, he summoned his family to Egypt to avoid starvation. They numbered about 70 when they arrived. Pharaoh, because of his love for Joseph, ordered that he and his family settle on the choicest land in the kingdom.

In the welcoming years, there was significant interaction and intermarriage between Israelites and Egyptians. Later, under the pharaoh "who knew not Joseph," the status of the Israelites deteriorated to the condition of slaves. Egyptian men began the practice of forcing themselves sexually on enslaved Hebrew women. Where have we heard that before?

The Exodus

The growing population of Hebrew slaves began to experience very oppressive working conditions. Their enslavement lasted for the greater part of 430 years. While there is serious disagreement among historians as to the exact size of the multitude that crossed the Red Sea with Moses, the range most acceptable to historians today is somewhere between 600,000 and one million. To be sure, this was a mixed multitude.

Were black folks among the multitude that crossed the Red Sea with Moses?

Since the Israelites, including Moses, were black and the Egyptians were black, everyone who crossed the Red Sea in the Exodus was black. The only difference between the Israelite slaves and their fellow Egyptian slaves was the gods they worshiped. At that time, they all, including the Israelites, worshiped many Gods.

The miracle in the desert

After 40 years in the desert and ongoing contact with the one true God, the rag-tagged mixed multitude united as one nation serving one God. They marched into the Promised Land as one people.

Who was Zipporah?

Zipporah, the future wife of one of the most famous men in the bible, was born in Africa somewhere between Ethiopia and Egypt. Her father, Jethro, was a Midian priest highly respected for his knowledge and wisdom. The Midianites were a group of people in Ethiopia made up of different tribes, all of whom were descendants of Midian, a son of Abraham and his later wife, Ketura.

Jethro was so appreciative of Moses for defending his seven daughters against bulling shepherd, that, despite religious differences, he gave Zipporah to Moses in marriage. This unexpected union produced two sons, Gershom and Eliezer. Jethro was also impressed with the intelligence of Moses, so much so that he appointed him guardian and superintendent over his substantial herd of cattle. This was all great news for Moses, a fugitive on the run from Egypt in need of a j.o.b. and a safe place to lay his head.

1. What did Moses' siblings think of his wife, Zipporah?
2. Was her race of concern to them?
3. Was Moses' marriage considered an interracial one?

We learn in Num. 12:1 that "Miriam and Aaron spoke against Moses because of the Ethiopian woman whom he had married." Putting aside this disagreement for a moment, it is quite clear from the Bible that Moses married and had two sons with an African woman. It is also clear that God showed no interest in Moses' choice of a wife. I would argue that Zipporah's race was really not an issue to Moses' siblings simply because the whole family were people of color.

That is why, contrary to what some would have us believe, Moses and Zipporah were not an interracial couple. To be sure, there were some cultural and religious differences, but race played no part in this little family squabble. In fact, there was no such concept as race in the world at that time. It was a later European invention around the year 1600.

What then was the real issue?

The real issue was the special authority and access that God granted to Moses and not to them. Num. 12:2 says, "has the Lord only spoken through Moses, they asked? Hasn't He also spoken through us? And the Lord heard this." God showed his anger at this pridefulness and criticism by striking Miriam's skin white with leprosy. (Why not also strike Aaron?)

Did God ever threaten to kill his faithful servant Moses?

After God speaks to Moses through a burning bush, Moses sets out with his family to return to Egypt. Exodus 4:24: "At a lodging place on the way, a strange incident occurred. The Lord met Moses and was about to kill him." God was angry with Moses for not circumcising his son as required by the covenant he had established with Abraham. Gen 17:9: "This is my covenant with you and your descendants after you, the covenant you are to keep, every male among you shall be circumcised."

Why do you think Moses' reluctance or refusal to circumcise his son engendered such anger in God that he was willing to kill him?

The covenant with Abraham does not call for such extreme action. It simply requires that a man with uncircumcised flesh is to be cut off from his people. But clearly, God was holding his faithful servant Moses to a much higher standard. By threatening his life, God wanted to impress upon Moses the seriousness of disobedience, especially in one who would be given the awesome responsibility of leading his people out of captivity and into the Land of the Promised. It was essential in God's sight that Moses' leadership and behavior be consistent with God's righteous commandments and covenants.

Given all the above, what did Moses do in response to God's anger?

1. Did he circumcise his son immediately?
2. Did he plead with God to allow the child to remain uncircumcised?
3. Did he continue to show no interest in circumcising his son? *
4. None of the above.

The Bible records no reaction whatsoever on the part of Moses to God's anger. Why then, did God not take his life?

There is also something to be said about a possible reluctance on the part of Zipporah to allow the circumcision of her son. Zipporah was aware of the Egyptian practice of circumcision, which dates back to at least 2400 BC. This practice was usually confined to the priesthood and the royal family. It is possible that Zipporah viewed the practice of circumcision as barbaric and wanted no part of it for her son. Her reaction after the circumcision of Gershom gives us an indication of her possible revulsion at the practice.

Sensing God's anger at their son not being circumcised, Zipporah took quick action. She picked up a flint stone and, to the extreme displeasure of her son, cut off his foreskin. Exodus 4:25: "Ziporah took a flint knife, cut of her son's foreskin and touched Moses' feet with it. 'Surely you are a bridegroom of blood to me,' she said." There is no question but that Zipporah's quick action saved Moses' life. It was a critical moment because the entire fate of the nation of Israel was in the hands of this black Ethiopian woman. Without her decisive action, the history of the Jewish people might have been significantly different.

Who was Thabis?

The Jewish historian Josephus provides us with the following account of Moses' first wife, Thabis. She was the daughter of the king of Ethiopia. In 1544 BC, a young Moses, heir to the throne of Egypt, led the pharaoh's army into battle against their Ethiopian neighbors. Thabis was so captivated by Moses' good looks and fearlessness in battle that she fell deeply in love with him and agreed to hand over the Ethiopian capital city on condition that he take her as his wife. (How's that for love and treachery at the same time?) He accepted her offer, and when he had succeeded in taking possession of the city, he honored his commitment and took Thabis as his wife. When the war was over, Thabis wanted Moses to remain in Ethiopia, but he insisted upon returning to Egypt. Later, when he was forced to flee from Egypt, he did not return to Ethiopia to retrieve Thabis.

CHAPTER FOURTEEN

The Bible is the Black Man's History #3

Who is this famous Black sister of the Bible?
I'm going to read to you a factual statement about a famous black woman in the Bible. I will give you a few minutes to think about who she is. You are all familiar with the biblical accounts of these women.

1. This black sister requested that 10 men be killed, and they were — Esther (real name Hadassah)
   - She was a descendant of Benjamin, Jacob's youngest black son.
   - Her family was carried off into captivity by Nebuchadnezzar's army in 597 BC. At the end of the 70-year period, her family chose to remain in the land of captivity rather than return to Jerusalem.
   - She is revealed in the Bible as a self-sacrificing woman of clear judgment, magnificent self-control, and loyalty.
   - However, below that beautiful face and keen intelligence was a vindictive heart. She petitioned her husband, the king, to have the ten sons of Haman (her uncle's enemy) hanged and it was done. She also petitioned the king to set aside a period of

time when her Jewish brethren could dole out vengeance upon the people who had been given license to kill them. (The Jews then proceeded to kill thousands.) Obviously, Esther had not learned to love her enemies.

2. The firstborn child of this famous black sister died shortly after its birth — Bathsheba (The one who liked to bath in public view)
   - Bathsheba was a black Canaanite. (Canaan is the ancient name for the country we call Palestine today.) Her father, Eliam, was from the city of Giloh which is in the southern part of Palestine.
   - Her grandfather Ahithophel was one of King David's most trusted Generals.
   - In addition to being King Solomon's mother, Bathsheba had three other sons for King David: Shimea, Shobab, and Nathan (I wonder if Nathan was named after the prophet Nathan who pointed out David's adulterous behavior.)

Let's explore some troubling concerns about sister Bathsheba's behavior and motives.
   - Given the physical layout of the area and the closeness of her home to the palace, Bathsheba must have known that her outside bathing routine was observable from the palace. Now I ask you, **how complicit was the sister?**
   - She may have also had intelligence from her husband that the king was in the palace. Her husband, Uriah, was a loyal soldier in the king's army and knew David was no longer leading his men in battle. Although he was away at war, he may have shared that intelligence with his wife before departing. Again, I ask you: **How complicit was the sister?**
   - Why didn't Bathsheba exhibit courage like Queen Vashi of the Book of Esther and refuse to lie with King David? Up to that point, King David walked with and feared the Lord. I think

it was highly unlikely at that time that he would have forced her to lie with him against her will. **How complicit was the sister?**
- Bathsheba grew up in a Canaanite culture where women were equal to men, which was in sharp contrast to the subservient position of women in the Hebrew culture. Objecting to King David's advances would not have upset any cultural norms on her part. **How complicit was the sister?**
- Did Bathsheba know or suspect that King David's guilt at making her pregnant could or would lead him to kill her husband, and if she knew, did she plead for her husband's life? **How complicit was the sister?**

3. This black sister protected her future husband and his associate from extreme danger — Rahab (the Harlot)
   - Rahab was an Amorite, a descendant of Canaan, the black son of Ham.
   - Her name means insolence or fierceness.
   - She came from a people who worshiped many gods.
   - She became familiar with the religion of the Israelites and soon accepted Jehovah as the one true God.
   - When she cleaned up her act, she married one of the spies that Joshua had sent to spy out the Promised Land, one of the two men she sheltered and protected.
   - She became the mother of Boaz, who married Ruth; their son, Obed, was the father of Jesse, who was King David's father.
   - Rahab, the prostitute is listed as an ancestor of Jesus in St. Mathew's genealogy.

4. This black sister was a seeker of wisdom and truth and didn't mind traveling extensively to be educated — The Queen of Sheba (Sheba was a great city in Ethiopia)

- Makeda was her real name. She had a keen, penetrating mind and was a seeker of wisdom and truth, and she set about on a journey of discovery.
- Ethiopian archives report that the Queen of Sheba was a monarch who ruled the Axumite empire, which included northern Ethiopia and parts of Egypt.
- Prior to her voyage to Jerusalem, she heard that Solomon's remarkable wisdom was due to the blessings of his God.
- The union of Solomon and the Queen of Sheba produced a son named Menelik. He was the ancestor of today's royal family in Ethiopia. Yes, the great Ethiopian leader Haile Selassie called by some "The Lion of Judah" was a descendant of Solomon's son Menelik.
- Having a child with a neighboring monarch was not an unusual event because it often resulted in generations of peace between the two nations.
- Apparently, Solomon loved his son Menelik, because he had him brought to Jerusalem to be educated in the finest schools.

5. This black sister flipped the script on her father-in-law — Tamar was the daughter-in-law of Judah and a Canaanite woman.
    - Tamar married two of Judah's sons. Unfortunately, both of them died before fathering any children with her.
    - Tamar was ultimately more righteous than Judah.
    - She knew that Judah never intended to follow the custom and give her his last son in marriage.
    - Her creative solution was motivated by her desire to retain the family inheritance and name through her children, which would have happened had one of her deceased husbands fathered a child with her.
    - Through her union with Judah, she gave birth to twin sons.

- Jesus Christ is the bloodline descendant of Tamar and Judah's son, Perez (see Matt 1:3).
6. This beautiful black sister rejected the marriage offer of the most widely admired king in the world — The Shulamite Woman of the "Song of Solomon"
    - She was a black peasant girl who had a wise perspective on love.
    - First of all, you must realize that "Song of Solomon" is a story about a choice in love. This peasant girl is presented with such a choice: marry King Solomon or a shepherd boy.
    - She is a country girl who works hard maintaining her vineyard. She has fallen in love with a neighboring shepherd boy. At one point, because of her great beauty, she is brought to the tents of Solomon to be groomed as one of his wives.
    - Solomon tells her that she is more beautiful than any of his 60 wives and 80 concubines. But the words that stirred her heart most were the simple words of her beloved shepherd boy: "You are beautiful, my darling, beautiful beyond words." And, "Your breasts are like two fawns, twin fawns of a gazelle grazing in a field of lilies."
    - While being told how beautiful she is by Solomon and the women around him, she repeatedly asks that they not rush her into making a choice. She pleaded, "Do not stir up nor awaken love until it pleases." This young woman exemplified for young people how intimacy can be looked forward to with delight and anticipation but still be saved for the marriage bed.
7. This black sister was the queen that everyone loved to hate — Jezebel was the daughter of Ethbaal, the king and high priest of the Canaanite cities of Tyre and Sidon.

- She was a powerful, determined woman who was a trusted advisor to her husband, the king. She became so dominant in the palace that she was able to bend his will to hers.
- Jezebel was deeply religious and refused to relinquish her beliefs and submit to her husband. Instead, she brought Baal worship into the royal palace and even persuaded the king to turn from the true God to worship Baal.
- Jezebel's superior intelligence was only matched by her ruthlessness and cunning, but think about it. We could say the same thing about King David. While not condoning the behavior of either, Jezebel had a man killed in order to steal his property; King David had a man killed in order to steal his wife.
- Jezebel's domination of King Ahab was so widely known that she became the feared commander of Israel.
- As we piece together the world from Jezebel's perspective, a fuller picture of this incredible woman begins to emerge. Phoenician and Canaanite women enjoyed enormous liberty and were regarded as the equal of men. For example, both men and women presided equally over religious ceremonies. As the daughter and only child of the king and high priest, Jezebel, had she stayed in Sidon, would have been her father's successor. Perhaps now you can better understand her resistance and defiance of the male-dominated world into which she had married.
- Jezebel was not a prostitute as some modern-day historians would have us believe. She came from and married into royalty.

So now you know that hidden in plain sight in the Bible are some extraordinary black women.

The Black Madonnas

I was totally surprised and dumbfounded when, in Spain, I discovered that there was such a thing as a Black Madonna. The Madonna that I encountered in Spain was the Black Virgin of Monserrat located in Barcelona. The faces of both Mary and the baby Jesus were black.

Who or what are the Black Madonnas?
The term Black Madonna Refers to statues and portraits of the Blessed Virgin Mother holding the infant Jesus in her arms. As mentioned earlier, the faces of both mother and child are depicted as black. There are hundreds of these Black Madonnas in churches throughout Europe: in Spain, France, Italy, Switzerland, Poland, Lithuania, Czechoslovakia, Russia, etc. They all date back to before the Middle Ages.

The Black Madonnas in these locations are highly revered by local worshipers because of the countless miracles attributed to them. These Black statues and paintings of the Blessed Mother and Child are not officially recognized by the Catholic Church, although Popes and other high-ranking church officials make regular pilgrimages to worship at the shrines of Black Madonnas. It is anyone's guess how they justify worshiping images of both white and black Blessed Mothers.

Our Lady of Vladimir, one of the Black Madonna in Russia, shows a black baby Jesus with happy-to-be nappy hair.

What is the significance of the continuing existence of the Black Madonnas?
The continued existence of the Black Madonnas is significant because their very presence transforms the churches and shrines in which they are located into sacred, hallowed grounds. Extreme care is given to their safety, security, and upkeep.

Many of the Madonna statues were created centuries ago, some as early as the 12th or 13th centuries. Their historical significance and religious notoriety have withstood the test of time, as they are still widely celebrated and worshiped. The Catholic church, which does not publicly acknowledge the existence of the Black Madonnas, is cautious not to advocate their removal or destruction.

What do you think are some of the reasons given by Whites to explain the blackness of the Madonnas?

1. The images were darkened by smoke from candlelight or accidental fires. (This is what I was told in Spain.) While on the surface, this appears plausible, it was unlikely to happen because none of the caretakers would allow candles close enough to the sacred statues to cause fires or burn marks.
2. It is claimed that the Madonnas were darkened because they were buried in the earth to save them from destruction by enemies. It is alleged that chemicals and paint from the statues interacted with the soil, and this caused the blackness. Surely the sacred statues were not buried without sufficient insulation wrapping. (This is truly a bit of a stretch.)
3. Some statutes are made of black ebony or other dark woods. I would say that ebony wood was chosen specifically because they intended the images to be black. If you want a white Madonna, it's probably not a good idea to use naturally black wood.
4. Some Black Madonnas were painted in the "Byzantine style," which usually depicted biblical characters as dark. (The Byzantine Empire was the Eastern European wing of the Roman Empire and the Roman Church.) The Byzantines believed that the Jews of that era were people of color.

5. The medieval custom of bathing statues in wine could also have contributed to the darkening of the Madonnas. Well, I would guess that even statues need a little taste once in a while.
6. The Black Madonnas were originally white but became black because of age and environmental conditions. The exact environmental conditions that contributed to this alleged discoloration are not detailed.

In conclusion, we have just gone through six frequently used excuses to explain the color of the Black Madonnas. To borrow a phrase from Shakespeare, "me think thee protesteth too loudly." The simplest and most logical reason for the blackness of the Madonnas is that Mary and Jesus were black, and the ancient artists portrayed them as they knew them to be.

An additional conclusion that is hard to avoid is that if you accept and revere a Black Blessed Mother, you must also accept and revere her Black child, who is Jesus Christ.

Did you know that one of the gospel writers of the New Testament painted images of Jesus' mother? (Which Gospel writer do you think this was?) In the Middle Ages, many noted clergymen argued that Mary must have been dark-skinned because that's how the Gospel writer St. Luke portrayed her in famous icons and statues.

I wonder why the subject of Black Madonnas is never discussed or preached from the pulpits in the Black Churches.

Part Four

AN UNCOMFORTABLE TRUTH ABOUT JESUS OF NAZARETH

CHAPTER FIFTEEN

An uncomfortable Truth about Jesus of Nazareth #1

Let me start this presentation with a statement for which there has never been any disagreement or controversy: Jesus Christ of Nazareth was a black African. Well, now that I have your attention, let me proceed by presenting what I consider to be a carefully thought-out and researched exploration into the physical life of the man Jesus, the one who walked among us for 33 years doing the work of his heavenly Father.

Before we proceed, however, tighten your seat belts because most of what you read will be unfamiliar and may even clash with the teachings you have been exposed to all your life.

Our inquiry will not include an exploration of the divinity of Jesus. I am in complete accord with Peter, who said that Jesus is "the Christ, the Son of the living God" (Matt 16:16).

After a little background info, I would like to start the journey into the life of the physical Jesus with a brief look at some of his ancestors. Since, according to the Bible, after the flood, the human race started anew with Noah and his family, that would be a good place to start.

For starters, let's have a look at the Garden of Eden.
Earlier, we presented archaeological and DNA evidence proving that the Garden of Eden was in fact located in Africa. As a consequence, it is reasonable to conclude that Adam and Eve were Africans. People born in Africa are usually thought of as Africans.

There were only nine generations between the death of Adam and the construction of Noah's Ark. Except for an occasional albino, neither historians nor anthropologists have been able to uncover any evidence to support the existence of a white population in Noah's era. If there were indeed white people on earth during Noah's lifetime, a good question to be asked is where did they come from?

Is it possible for white couples to produce black offspring?
According to Western history revisionists, Noah had one black son, his youngest son Ham. How did Noah and Mrs. Noah produce this one black child when, according to these same revisionists, the other sons were white? Well, let's go to the videotape and see if there is any evidence to support this creative myth. Today's scientists, in a rare demonstration of unanimity, agree that black couples can and often do produce fair or white offspring. However, they are equally persuaded that it is genetically impossible for white couples to produce dark-skinned offspring. Therefore, Noah, Mrs. Noah, or both would have had to have been black to produce this one black child.

The same reasoning can be applied to Adam and Eve. Following the above scientific data to its logical conclusion, if Adam and Eve were white, they would only be able to produce white offspring. Then the question to be asked would be where did the black folks come from?

Now let's have a look at Noah, the first father after the flood, who loved his God and loved his wine. (Why did I say Noah loved his wine? Gen 9:20-21: "Noah, a man of the soil, proceeded to plant a vineyard. When he drank some of its wine, he became drunk...")

Before we delve into the life of Noah, I would like to share a bit of trivia: who was Noah's grandaddy? Hint: he walked the earth longer than Adam. (Methuselah.)

Noah, who was ordained a priest at the tender age of 10, was considered by God to be a righteous man of unshakable faith. He did not question God's command to build a large boat in the middle of the desert although everyone in his village was convinced that he was delusional (Gen. 6:14-16). His three sons were pressed into the Ark-building service as free labor.

Was it possible that Noah was an albino?
There is some evidence to suggest that Noah was albino. Witness Noah's daddy's reaction when seeing his son for the first time. He observed that the baby's body was "white as snow and red as the blooming of a rose, and the hair on his was white like wool, and with long locks" (from the Dead Sea Scrolls). There is only one group of people on the planet who can wear their hair in long, wooly locks, and that is the Africans. Therefore, Noah may have been an Albino, but his genes were definitely African.

In the Bible, God instructs Noah's descendants to increase and fill the Earth. Gen 9:1: "Then God blessed Noah and his sons, saying to them, Be fruitful and increase in number and fill the earth." Therefore, in obedience to God, Noah's offspring populated the entire post-flood world with black and brown offspring.

Noah's sons and their descendants
Shem's descendants are associated with the ancient countries located in what we now call the Middle East: Palestine, Syria, Iraq, etc. Shem

is a direct ancestor of Abraham, the father of the Hebrew lineage, which includes the bloodline of Jesus Christ. The world's three great religions sprang from Shem's descendants: Judaism, Christianity and Islam.

Noah's "forgotten" son is Japheth; the Bible makes minimal mention of Japheth or his offspring. Japheth's descendants migrated to Eastern Europe. He is celebrated in the Western world as "the father of the Caucasian race." His descendants were originally people of color. However, according to one theory, time, mutations, limited sunlight, and the frigid climates of Eastern Europe, gradually turned their skin white and hair straight. These descendants settled initially in the Caucasus region of Eastern Europe, which included Turkey, Russia, Armenia, Georgia, and parts of Iran. Some time later they migrated into Western Europe: England, France Italy, Spain, etc.

Ham, the father of mighty nations
The sons of Ham, for the most part, settled in North Africa and created great nations and mighty kingdoms. Other members of the clan migrated to more distant parts of the world (including China, Australia, and even the Americas), bringing technical innovations and cultural sophistication everywhere they went. Can anyone tell me where Han's descendants settled in China? The Yellow River Delta in southwest China.

Who was the first Hebrew and father of many nations?
Abraham was a descendant of Noah's oldest son, Shem, and a direct descendant of Shem's great-grandson, Elber (or Heber, from where the word Hebrew is thought to have been derived). Heber and his family lived in the country of Canaan.

Abraham's father, Terah, lived in the bustling city of Ur, which was the center of a wealthy Samaritan city-state located in Northeast

Africa. Ancient Ur was part of the city-state empire built by Nimrod, the black grandson of Ham and the builder of the Tower of Babel.

Why was age just a number to Father Abraham?
Although Abraham got a late start, he took the title of Father seriously. He fathered children by three black women: Sarah from Ur (the bustling city in Northeast Africa as mentioned above), Hagar from Egypt, and Keturah, whose origin in Africa is uncertain. The "late in life" union between Abraham and Keturah produced six sons, all of whom became the fathers of Arab nations. Keturah has been called by Rabbinic scholars "the most ignored significant person in the Bible." Also under the radar in the Bible is the fact that Abraham fathered these six sons at the advanced age of 140. There was a rumor going around in Ur that Father Abraham was wolfing down Viagra and testosterone pills.

The offspring of Keturah contributed to the fulfillment of the promise that God made Abraham to make him "the father of many nations." Thirty families came from Abraham in total: twelve chieftains of Arab nations from Ishmael and sixteen chieftains of Arab nations from Keturah's sons, and let us not forget the Israelite nations.

Another interesting bit of trivia: Abraham's ancestor, Shem, lived to the ripe old age of 600, was still alive when Abraham was born, and outlived Abraham by 35 years.

Jacob's son Joseph, the teenager whose dream cost him his freedom
In order to have a meaningful discussion of Joseph and the significance of his life to the biblical narrative, we need to first establish a little something about Egypt. The country of Egypt is mentioned in some 588 verses and 32 books in the Bible, which confirms its importance to the biblical story. The Egyptians of the Bible, especially in the Old Testament, were black Africans. They were descendants of Noah's baby boy Ham.

Jacob's favorite son, Joseph, was considered a high-ranking Egyptian official by his brothers when they went to Egypt to purchase grain for the family. They were unaware that the official who stood before them was none other than the sibling that they had sold into slavery. He recognized them immediately, but they did not recognize him (Gen. 42:6-7). Joseph had grown to manhood and to his siblings appeared indistinguishable from any other black Egyptian officials.

Moses, the Lawgiver
When Pharaoh's daughter plucked baby Moses out of the Nile, she immediately became attached to him and determined in her heart to keep him and raise him as her son. She was well aware that the infant was a Hebrew child (Exodus 2:6). The princess was further determined to have her father, the pharaoh, accept this child as his grandson and heir to his throne. Would the ruler of the most powerful country in the world accept a Hebrew child as his grandson and heir if that child did not look like him and his people, especially since this pharaoh recently issued an edict calling for the death of all male Hebrew newborns (Exodus 1:15-16)?

A SURPRISING WITNESS
In 1939, the father of modern psychoanalysis, Sigmund Freud, wrote a book entitled *Moses and Monotheism*. In this amazing little book, Freud carefully documented, among other surprising revelations, that Moses, the "law giver" of the Bible was a black Egyptian.

Some clarification of terms before we move on.

1. A Hebrew is a descendant of Abraham.
2. An Israelite is a descendant of Jacob and/or his 12 sons.
3. A Shemite is a descendant of Noah's oldest son, Shem.
4. A Semite is a member of a people speaking one of the African family of Semitic languages: the Arabs, Hebrews, Arameans,

Babylonians, Canaanites, Carthaginians, and more; all are Semitic peoples. The word Semite does not appear anywhere in the Bible.
5. What then, is the definition of a Jew? A Jew in the Bible is a descendant of the tribe of Judah. A Jew outside of the Bible is someone who converted to, or whose ancestors converted to, the religion of Judaism.

Question: Which of the two types of Jews mentioned above describes the majority of Jews in Israel today? I would argue that it is the second definition.

Were the children of Israel also children of the "Mother Land"? If so, is there any evidence?

1. If you look up Amos 9:7 in your Bible, you will see that God himself calls the Israelites black. "Are you not the children of the Ethiopians unto me, O children of Israel?"
2. Jacob's favorite son, Joseph, rose to become the second in command in Egypt. When his brothers saw him, they assumed that he was a black Egyptian official.
3. Josephus, a Jewish historian born four years after the death of Christ, wrote that "both the Israelites and the Egyptians were black."
4. The Roman historian Tacitus, writing around the year 100 AD (77 years after the crucifixion of Christ), said that "the Jews are a race of Ethiopian origin."
5. When Joseph buried his father, Jacob, he and his family observed a seven-day mourning period. (GEN 50:11) "When the Canaanites, who lived there saw the mourning, they said, the Egyptians are holding a solemn ceremony of mourning."

The Canaanites assumed that they were looking upon a group of black Egyptians.
6. The Assyrians have sculptured wall reliefs that depict captive Israelites in chains with wooly hair and African facial features.

Were Black women also ancestors of Jesus?

1. Mary – the teenage mother of Jesus. She was born and raised in the Canaanite city of Bethlehem. She was also a descendant of one of King David and Bathsheba's sons, Nathan. Additional proof is provided by the existence of hundreds of Black Madonna statues and portraits throughout Europe depicting the Blessed Mother and Child as Black.
2. Rahab – the prostitute who saved the lives of Joshua's spies. She was a Canaanite woman (a descendant of Noah's son, Ham). She became the mother of Boaz, who married Ruth (a Moabite). Their son, Obed, was the father of Jesse, who was the father of King David.
3. Tamar – also a Canaanite woman. Her union with Judah (Gen.38) resulted in the birth of twin sons, one of whom, Pharez or Perez, is listed in Matthew's genealogy of Jesus.
4. Bathsheba – the Hittite/Canaanite wife of King David and mother of King Solomon and three other sons. One of these three sons, Nathan (as mentioned above), is in Luke's lineage of the blessed mother.

While none of what we have discussed so far can be considered scientific-grade proof, the evidence presented is overwhelming and makes a very strong case for the Israelites of the Old Testament and the ancestors of Jesus being something other than white.

What was the response of the Romans and other European rulers to the fledgling Christian church?

Before 312 AD, European rulers, especially in Rome, were extremely brutal toward Christians and Christianity. As a consequence, Christians had to endure centuries of horrendous persecution. An untold number of martyrs suffered excruciating torture and death. In an effort to escape the carnage in Rome, many Christians fled to other countries. Where do you think the majority of these fleeing Christians went?

It is well-documented that the majority of the Christians fleeing Rome at that time went to countries in Africa. Why Africa? If they were white, why didn't they flee to another white country?

In a similar situation some 242 years earlier in 70 AD, when the Romans utterly destroyed Jerusalem and laid to waste its magnificent temple (as foretold by Jesus), over a million Jews were killed in the massacre. The majority of those fleeing sought refuge in African countries. Again, why African countries?

What brought about the end of the Roman persecution of Christians?

In the fourth century, something extraordinary happened. The Roman emperor Constantine converted to Christianity. He established Christianity as the official religion of the Roman Empire. Suddenly, Christianity became an accepted worldwide religion. The newly-formed Roman church under Emperor Constantine made radical changes to sacred Christian doctrines.

Constantine immediately set about implementing self-serving additions and revisions to traditional Christian doctrine, such as:

1. Sinful worshipers were now required to pay money for the forgiveness of their sins.

2. He demanded that church leaders address his concerns regarding the African appearance of noted biblical personalities.

3. He issued a number of rulings that resulted in greater privileges and responsibilities for bishops, who then became his ambassadors and enforcers.

4. He presided over the Council of Nicaea, where the concept of the Holy Trinity was codified.

The hijacking of Christianity by the Europeans changed it from a small group of devotees following a wise and holy Jewish prophet (Jesus) to an enormous ethnocentric pyramid of Christian dominance with Caucasians perched at the top..

CHAPTER SIXTEEN

An uncomfortable truth about Jesus of Nazareth #2

Is it important for us to know the physical appearance of Jesus?

The Bible is filled with non-physical descriptions of Christ that speak mainly to the impact of his divinity:

- The light of the world
- The good shepherd
- The bright morning star
- The way, the truth, and the life
- The high priest
- The author and perfector of our faith

While the above descriptions are manna to our souls and fuel to our faith, there is something that these statements do not provide. They do not provide a physical description of the man Jesus. At this point, I think we should ask ourselves how important is it for us to know the physical appearance of Jesus. Would such information add anything significant to the New Testament story? I feel certain that the New Testament writers would have reported Jesus' physical appearance as a matter of fact if they deemed it critical to the telling of the Gospel story.

Given that these authors saw no need to discuss the physical appearance of Jesus, how did we become so overwhelmed with images of a white Jesus?

Does the Bible provide any physical descriptions of Jesus?

While it is true that the Bible does not provide a specific description of the physical Jesus, it is not silent on the issue. Numerous descriptions of Jesus can be found in the Old Testament. Let's review a few:

1. Revelation 1:13 -15 NLT: "And standing in the middle of the lampstands was someone like the Son of Man. He was wearing a long robe with a gold sash across his chest. His head and his hair were like wool, as white as snow. And his eyes were like flames of fire. His feet were like polished bronze refined in a furnace."
2. Daniel 10:5-6 NLT: "I looked up and saw a man dressed in linen clothing, with a belt of pure gold around his waist. His body looked like a precious stone gem. His face flashed like lightning and his eyes flamed like torches. His arms and feet shone like polished bronze."
3. Daniel 7:9 NLT: "I watched as thrones were put in place and the Ancient One sat down to judge. His clothing was as white as snow, his hair like pure wool."
4. Also, see Isaiah 53.

While the above scriptures are highly suggestive of a Black Jesus, they leave a lot of room for discussion and debate. However, none of them describe the white Jesus so prevalent on TV, in printed material, and in the movies. Today, virtually every statue or painting of Jesus found in Western churches, literature, movies, and printed material exhibits a standardized white image of our Savior.

"Out of Egypt I have called my son," says Mat 2:15-16 NIV, "When they had gone, an angel of the lord appeared to Joseph in a dream. Get up he said, take the child and his mother and escape to Egypt. Stay there until I tell you, for Herod is searching for the child to kill him."

If Joseph and his family were white, it is unlikely that God would have instructed them to hide out among black Egyptians, where they would easily be recognized as foreigners.

Are there any credible sources outside of the Bible that describe the physical Jesus?

This will be the most controversial part of the presentation, so I need you to pay close attention. While it is true that the Bible does not provide us with an exact description of the incarnate Jesus, the Jewish historian Josephus does. Flavius Josephus was born only four years after the end of Jesus' earthly ministry and is considered the most credible and influential historian of that era.

Josephus claimed to have had special access to Roman records and documents from which he gained special knowledge and insight into the Jewish prophet, Jesus.

Josephus wrote the following text describing the physical Jesus only a few decades after the Savior's crucifixion. It appears to be the oldest and, quite possibly, the most authentic description of Jesus in existence:

"At that time also there appeared a certain man of magic powers... If it be meet to call him a man, whose name is Jesus, whom (certain) Greeks call a son of (a) god, but his disciples (call) the true prophet... He was a man of simple appearance, mature age, Black-skinned, short growth, three cubits

(or 4 feet, 5 inches tall), **hunchbacked, with a long face, a long nose, eyebrows meeting above the nose, curly hair, but having a line in the middle of the head after the fashion of the Nazarenes, with an undeveloped beard."**

Do you think the above text is credible? If yes, why? If not, why?
One factor that strongly points to the credibility of Josephus's text is the extent to which Western church leaders went to discredit him and rewrite his text. If they thought the text was a fabrication, they would have simply ignored it.

Also, as mentioned earlier, the Josephus text was written only a few decades after the end of Jesus' ministry on earth. At that time, John, who calls himself "the apostle whom Jesus loved" was still alive, as were many other unnamed disciples who had walked with Jesus. Having firsthand knowledge, any one of them could have spoken against the Josephus text. There is no evidence that any of them ever did.

What was the reaction of Western church leaders to the Josephus text?
They were outraged and very uncomfortable with their Jesus being described as black-skinned, hunched back, and physically unattractive. These and other portions of Josephus's text were deemed offensive and copies of it were unceremoniously rounded up and destroyed. Further, if they truly believed that the Josephus text was inauthentic, why would they go through the trouble of publishing so many carefully worded counterfeit versions of it?

As a consequence, for more than 1,500 years, no copy of the original Josephus text could be found anywhere in Europe. The numerous rewrites were so extensive that they bore very little resemblance to the original.

Just when it seemed that an original, unadulterated copy of the Josephus text would never be found, in 1931, scholar Robert Eisler discovered among the archives of ancient Russian church documents an uncorrupted copy of the Josephus text. This discovery validates Dr. Martin Luther King Jr's assertion that "truth thrust to the ground will rise again."

Let's examine one of the hundreds of published adulterated translations of the Josephus text.

This text was taken from the magazine *Jewish Antiquities* and translated by Louis H. Felder. **"About this time there lived Jesus, a wise man, if indeed one ought to call him a man. For he was one who performed surprising deeds. And was a teacher of such people as accepted the truth gladly. He won over many Jews and many Greeks. He was the Messiah. And when, upon the accusation of the principal men among us, Pilate had condemned him to the cross. Those who had first come to love him did not cease. He appeared to them spending a third day restored to life, for the prophets of God had foretold these things and a thousand other marvels about him. And the tribe of the Christians, so called after him, has still to this day not disappeared."**

While this revision is reassuring to the faithful and provides an inspired retelling of the life, death, and resurrection of the man Jesus, it is nonetheless a shameless corruption of the original Josephus text.

What appears to be omitted from this revised text?

It omits any mention of the meticulous physical description of Jesus provided by Josephus.

The mysterious, illusive images of Jesus

There were no portraits of Jesus made during his lifetime. Therefore, the countless images of Jesus that overwhelm us today were formed exclusively by the imagination of the artist who produced them.

From the very first time Christian children (black and white) attend Sunday School, an image of Jesus Christ is etched into their little minds. That image is of a tall man with long flowing hair, white skin, and soft-colored eyes (frequently blue). While such an image is pervasive today, it does not describe a person who lived in the tropical region of the world where Jesus was born. If it were true that a white-complexioned Jesus lived out his entire life in a land of black and brown people, it certainly would not have escaped the notice of the New Testament writers.

A recent groundbreaking scientific project created a computerized model of a man living during Jesus' time and in the same location where he was born.

A new and exciting science called forensic anthropology has emerged on the scene. Its focus is the recreation of the facial features of ancient people. This scientific breakthrough relies heavily on anatomy, anthropology, digital imagery, and many other high-tech modalities.

As part of a recent study, a team of forensic anthropologists under the leadership of Professor Richard Neave from the University of Manchester, England successfully recreated what they believe is an accurate three-dimensional bust of a man living at the same time as Jesus and in the same geographic location. The team's recreation resulted in an image of a brown-skinned man with Negroid features and curly hair.

Dr. Neave realized that the resulting model was not perfect. While the head and facial features were scientifically accurate, the color, texture, and length of the hair, as well as the skin color, were less scientific.

The researchers got some assistance from the Bible in determining the length of Jesus' hair. In I Corinthians 11:15, Paul writes, "If a man has long hair, it is a disgrace to him." It is highly unlikely that Paul would have written this if Jesus Christ, whom he had seen personally, had long hair.

The researchers also received some help with skin color by examining the paintings on the walls of the Roman Catacombs (more about this later).

In summary, a team of modern forensic anthropologists produced a three-dimensional, computerized model of a contemporary of Jesus, which showed him to have brown skin, Negroid features, and curly hair.

Why was the land of Canaan, where Jesus was born, loved and hated by God?
The country of Canaan is mentioned in the Bible over 160 times, clearly establishing its importance to the Biblical story. This choice region of Northeast Africa was settled by Canaan, the fourth son of Ham, and was occupied by his descendants for thousands of years before the arrival of the Israelites. There are still some Indigenous Canaanites living in this region.

God considered the land of Canaan to be prime real estate and called it "the land of milk and honey." He promised to give it to the descendants of Abraham as a reward for Abraham's faithfulness. Genesis 17:8: "The whole land of Canaan, where you now reside as a foreigner, I will give as an everlasting possession to you and your descendants after you; and I will be their God."

God's anger toward the Canaanites, as mentioned in the Bible, was due to their decadent behavior and worship of many Gods. It had nothing to do with skin color or a drunken grandfather's curse. (If you'll recall a naked, hungover Noah cursed his grandson, Canaan in Genesis 9:21.)

What countries occupy the land of Canaan today?
The ancient land of Canaan today is occupied by the modern states of Israel, Jordan, Lebanon, and Syria. (Why is it that we consider these countries to be in the "Middle East" instead of Northeast Africa, where they are geographically located? The truth is that "Middle East" is a made-up designation to keep from acknowledging Northeast Africa. If there is a "Middle East," where is "Middle West?")

If I were to tell you of someone who was born, raised, lived out his entire life, and died in America, wouldn't you naturally assume that he was an American? Jesus was born, raised, preached, suffered, and died in the land of Canaan which is in Africa. Why then is it not naturally assumed that he was an African?

The Bible does not mention any occasion where Jesus left the region of his birth except as a child when his parents took him to Egypt to escape from King Herod, who wanted to kill him.

Discovering hidden underground treasures in ancient Rome
The Roman Catacombs are ancient subterranean burial tunnels located in and around the city of Rome. These massive underground tunnels were built and used by Christians somewhere between the 2nd and 5th centuries.

At that time in Rome, Christians were not permitted to bury their dead within the city limits. As a consequence, they resorted to burying their dead in vast underground tunnels called catacombs. These underground cemeteries soon became sacred sites due to the number of high-ranking priests and canonized saints who were laid to rest within their walls.

True or False: Church leadership turned the sacred subterranean cemetery into a "cash cow."
The catacombs soon became a source of considerable income. In order to encourage visitation by the faithful and to fatten up the treasury,

the church commissioned local artists to decorate the walls of the tunnels with paintings of scriptural scenes and renowned Biblical personalities. Of course, a modest donation was collected. Paintings on the walls included images of Jesus, Daniel, Moses, Jonah, Jesus' disciples, and many more. All were painted as people of color; not necessarily black, but people of color.

The paintings in the Roman catacombs, which date back to the second century, leave very little doubt that early Church Fathers believed that prominent biblical notables, including Jesus, were people of color.

An image of Jesus painted in the Catacombs, labeled "The Good Shepherd" shows Jesus with brown skin, short curly hair, and clean-shaven. Another painting dubbed "The Last Supper" shows him in a similar manner with his disciples.

Amazingly, despite the importance of these catacombs to the life of the early church, with time, knowledge of them faded. As a result, the subterranean tombs were left undisturbed for many centuries. Today, there are about 40 Catacombs that we know of, but only a very few are open to the public. I wonder why?

The Russian Catacombs: More Underground Witnesses
The Russian Catacombs, like the Roman Catacombs, were subterranean cemeteries for the early Christians. Christians in the eastern corner of Europe were called the Byzantine. Unlike Western European Christians, Byzantine Christians were not inclined to alter the complexion of Jesus or other prominent biblical personages.

It was not surprising, therefore, that the images of Biblical greats on the walls of the Russian Catacombs were all painted with dark or brown complexions. The reason for this is simple: that is what they knew them to be..

CHAPTER SEVENTEEN

An uncomfortable truth about Jesus of Nazareth #3

As mentioned previously, there are over 500 Black Madonnas in churches throughout Western and Eastern Europe: in Spain, France, Italy, Switzerland, Poland, Lithuania, Czechoslovakia, etc. Actually, there were hundreds more but they were destroyed by advancing armies.

Napoleon Bonaparte, in a fit of uncontrolled bigotry and madness, commanded his troops to destroy hundreds of the sacred Black Madonnas when he marched through Europe. Apparently, the little dude was a racist.

Over the years and leading up to the present time, reverence for Black Madonnas has not diminished, which prompts me to ask the next question: why haven't white church leaders advocated for the removal or destruction of these black statues and portraits?

The Black Madonnas in Europe are held in the highest esteem by the faithful because of the countless miracles attributed to them. Christian leadership, for the most part, is very much aware of the existence and authenticity of these Madonnas, yet they are reluctant to officially recognize them or to advocate their removal or destruction. This presents an interesting dilemma.

If they remain silent, they will be tacitly acknowledging the authenticity of the 500 statues and portraits of the Black Madonnas and Black Baby Jesus. This option, however, does afford them a measure of deniability. The evil I don't see doesn't exist.

If they denied the authenticity of the Black Madonnas outright, they would have to explain why so many high-ranking church officials worship a white Mother of Jesus in public and a Black Mother of Jesus in private (more about this later).

Is anyone other than me wondering why Black church leadership never mentions the Black Madonnas?

True or False: Many Popes secretly worship black Madonnas.
Popes, for centuries, knew the truth about the Northeast (African) origin of Christianity. There is a small chapel located within the Vatican with a large portrait of a Black Madonna and a child situated regally on a high altar. This private chapel is never opened to the public. Popes and other high-ranking church officials regularly go to this chapel to worship the Black Madonna. Yes, they know the truth but are content to take that truth to their graves rather than reveal it to the faithful. Finally, someone (and I wish I could remember who) once said, "You can always tell the soundness of a truth by the army of lies that surround and protect it from being revealed."

The Birth of the White Jesus
Nowhere in the Bible can one find any language that speaks directly, or even indirectly, of a white Jesus. The movement to represent Jesus and the ancient Hebrews/Israelites as white first emerged during the Renaissance period between the 14th to the 17th centuries under the

leadership of Catholic popes, although there were white Jesus images painted as early as the sixth century.

Pope Alexander VI, the fornicating Pope

Rodrigo Borgia became Pope Alexander VI in 1492. He was corrupt, worldly, and ambitious. From the very start, he displayed dissatisfaction with images of a Jewish, African-looking Jesus. So, in order to create a more "European-looking" Jesus, he commissioned the great artists of his day to paint an image of Jesus that resembled a Caucasian. The Pope further required that his illegitimate son, Cesare, be the model for this white Jesus. There was fierce competition among the artists to present the Pope with the best portrait of a white, Cesare-looking Jesus. The Pope selected the painting rendered by Leonardo Da Vinci which was entitled, "Salvador Mundi" which means "savior of the world"

As the Supreme Pontiff and leader of the church in Rome, Pope Alexander set into motion a campaign to have the Catholic church accept Da Vinci's portrait of Cesare as the official "face of Jesus." And so it was. He then issued a Papal edict requiring the destruction of all existing art depicting a Semitic, colored Jesus.

True or False: The Pope's son, Cesare, was a God-fearing man.
Let's turn a spotlight on this Cesare Borgia, whose image was now the official "Face of Jesus."

1. As mentioned, Cesare was the illegitimate son of Pope Alexander VI. Cesare however, was not an only child; he was, in fact, one of four illegitimate children sired by the "Holy Father" and his mistress. So much for celibacy.
2. Cesare and his brother, Giovani, shared a mistress who just happened to be the wife of a third brother.

3. Because of extreme jealousy toward Giovani, Cesare was implicated in his brother's mysterious death.
4. Cesare and Leonardo da Vinci were so close that it was taken for granted that they were lovers.
5. Notwithstanding the above, he was also a notorious womanizer; he fathered 11 known illegitimate children with multiple women.
6. Cesare was not particularly choosy with his sexual partners. He had sex with his own sister, Lucrezia.

His father, Pope Alexander VI, was obviously more focused on changing the skin color of Jesus and promoting the image of his corrupt and immoral son than he was on advancing the Holy Word of God.

With Cesare's image as "the Face of Jesus," the faithful were duped into worshiping the devil. Yes, for centuries, the faithful worldwide were praying to and worshiping the image of this depraved, despicable Cesare Borgia, believing that his face was the image of the Holy Son of God.

Pope Julius II

In May of 1508, Pope Julius II contracted with Michelangelo to paint a creation scene on the ceiling of the Sistine Chapel at the Vatican. Using my "sanctified imagination," I could hear Pope Julius II instructing Michelangelo to "paint a scene of the heavenly realm on the ceiling with images of people as God created them," then with an unequivocal and resolute voice stating, "and make them look like us." The artist complied with the Pope's wishes and used his family members as models. For instance, his cousin was the model for the image of Jesus.

Who painted the most famous and the most reproduced image of Jesus ever? In the early 1940s, commercial artist Warner Sallman painted a color image of the face of Jesus which he labeled "the Head of Christ." This color image of Jesus exploded on the world scene. It achieved a level of circulation and popularity the likes of which have never been equaled or duplicated. It was reproduced over 700,000 times and came to define what Jesus, the central figure of Christianity, looked like for millions of individuals and generations of believers.

The image in Salman's painting revealed a gentle-looking white Christ with soft blue eyes focused reverently toward the Heavens. His blond hair was draped in a gentle wave down to his shoulder. For countless devout Christians, this likeness is the image of the son of God.

Sallman's painting was very successfully marketed worldwide. It was seen on virtually everything and everywhere: on stained glass windows, prayer cloths, fans, calendars, hymnals, pencils, bookmarks, etc. It was also hung in churches, courtrooms, police stations, libraries, and schoolhouses, and was distributed to soldiers going into battle during WWII. Sallman's "Head of Christ," while a complete and total figment of his imagination, is still the most worshiped image of Jesus Christ today. We are in a sad state of affairs when millions of believers are holding sacred the creative imagining of a commercial artist.

A significant truth that must be brought to light is that there is no evidence anywhere that Jesus looked anything like the blue-eyed blond-haired Sallman image of Christ. Yes, it is true that we do not know exactly what Jesus looked like. However, Jesus' miraculous birth, his teaching/healing ministry, and his death all occurred in one of the hottest places on the planet. A place where the Indigenous population was, and still is people of color. Jesus and his family (who were born and raised in this part of the world) were included in that indigenous population.

The backlash to Sallman's and others' images of Christ began to emerge in the 1960s and 1970s. In the 1960s, Malcolm X and

Elijah Mohammed were the first to speak out against a white Jesus. "Jesus was not a Pale-Face," declared Malcolm X. In the 1970s, black intelligentsia realized that the image of a white Jesus was a gross misrepresentation of the historic Jesus, the sole purpose of which is to perpetuate white superiority and white dominance.

More recently, Civil Rights activist and reporter for the New York Daily News Shaun King declared that "all of the statues of the white European which they claim to be Jesus should come down... They are a form of white supremacy and always have been." He also remarked that stained glass windows and other images of a white Jesus must also be destroyed. They are "racist propaganda" and "a gross form of white supremacy."

Several black authors took up their pens and wrote books rejecting the authenticity of the ever-present white Jesus. Three of these books speak directly to the issue: *What Color Was Jesus* by William Mosley, *Jesus Is A Black Man* by T.C. Wanyanwu, and *Was Jesus Christ A Negro?* by John G. Jackson.

To quote Buddha (the enlightened one): "There are three things in life you can always count on: the rising of the Sun, the rising of the Moon, and the rising of truth."

It must be emphasized at this point that the current demand for the removal of images of a white Jesus is not a call to reject Christianity but a call to reject a racist revisionist Christianity designed to perpetuate a white ethnocentric lie.

Can white Christianity in America survive a Black Jesus?

Today, white Americans whose ancestors bought, sold, traded, raped, and killed black and brown people for hundreds of years in the name of a white Jesus could not, in my estimation, imagine or accept the possibility of Christ being anything other than white. The White Jesus is the cornerstone of American racism. In consideration of this nation's racist history, it is totally plausible that the reality of a Black Jesus would signal the end of Christianity for white Americans. It may very well come down to a question of what is more sacred to them: white supremacy or the love, message, and reality of our Lord and Savior Jesus Christ, whatever he looks like.

References

Black History Before Slavery

David Imhotep Ph.D., The First Americans Were Africans – Documented Evidence (Author House 09/20/2012)

David Imhotep Ph. D., The First Americans Were Africans – Revised (Author House 03/14/2017)

Ivan Van Sertima, African Presence in Early America. (Journal of African Civilizations Ltd. Inc. (1992)

Dr. Clyde Winters, African empires in Ancient America. (2013)

Dr. Clyde Winters, We Are Not Just Africans – The Black Native Americans (2015)

Michael Bradley, Dawn Voyage – The Black African Discovery of America. (Eworld Inc. 1992)

W. Val Chambers, Black Men Before Columbus (Eureka Press 1991)

John Henrik Clarke Christopher Columbus and the Afrikan Holocaust – Slavery and the Rise of European Capitalism. (Eworld Inc. 1998)

Empress Verdiacee, Return of The Ancient Ones – The Tue History Uncovered of the Washitaw Empire. (The Washitaw Moundbuilder's Publishing Company 2011)

Claudia Gellman Mink, Cahokia: City of the Sun (Cahokia Mounds Museum Society 1992)

Ancient Black Egypt

Robert Bauval & Thomas Brophy Ph.D., Black Genesis – The Prehistoric Origins of Ancient Egypt (Bear & Company 2011)

Ivan Van Sertima, Egypt Child of America (Journal of African Civilizations Ltd, Inc. 1995)

R.A. Jairazbhoy, Ancient Egyptians in Middle and South America. Ra Publications London 1981)

R.A. Jairazbhoy, Ancient Egyptians and Chinese in America (George Prior Associated Publishers LTD 1974)

Charles River Editors, The Ancient Nubians – The History of the Oldest Civilizations in Africa.

Cheikh Ant Diop, The African Origin of Civilization – Myth or Reality (Lawrence Hill Books 1974)

George G.M. James, Stolen Legacy (1954)

Black History Before Slavery – South of the Boarder

Ivan Van Sertima, The Came Before Columbus – The African Presence in Ancient America (Random House Trade Paperbacks 1976)

Paul Alfred Barton, A History of the African-Olmecs – Black Civilizations of America from Prehistoric Times to the Present Era. (1998)

Anu M'Bantu, The Aboriginal Black Olmec Civilization (Pomegranate Publishing, London (2019)

Richard A. Diehl, The Olmecs – Americas First Civilization (Thames & Hudson 2004)

Black History Before Slavery – Around the World

P. James Oliver, Mansa Musa and the Empire of Mali (2013)

Runoko Rashidi & Ivan Van Sertima, African Presence in Early Asia (Transaction Publishers 1985)

Dr. Clyde Winters, The Ancient Blacks of China (2018)

Runoko Rashidi, My Global Journeys in search of the African Presence (Black Classic Press 2017)

J.A. Rogers, Sex and Race Vol 1 (Helga M. Rogers 1967)

J.A. Rogers, 100 Amazing facts about the Negro with complete proof – A Short Cut to the World history of the Negro (Helga M. Rogers 1955)

Robin Walker, When We Ruled – The Ancient and Mediaeval History of Black Civilizations (Black Classic Press 2006)

Supreme Design, LLC., When the World was Black – The Untold History of the World's first Civilizations, Part One: Prehistoric Culture (Supreme Design Publishing 2013)

Supreme Design, LLC., When the World was Black – The Untold History of the World's First Civilization, Part Two: Ancient Civilizations (Supreme Design Publishing 2013)

Rudolph R. Windsor, From Babylon to Timbuktu – A History of Ancient Black Races including The Black Hebrews (Windsor's Golden series, 19th Edition 2003)

Born Power, The Original Man – A Historical Look Into Black History (Nubian Publishing 2018)

John Henrik Clarke, Cheikh Anta Diop and the new light on African History (Brawtley Press 2014)

Robin Walker, If You want to Learn Early African History, Start Here (Reklaw Education LTD London 2014, 2015)

Dr. Theron D. Williams, The Bible is Black History (Self-Publishing Services: Writers Tablet.org 2018)

Rev. Walter Arthur McCray, The Black presence in the Bible – Discovering the Black and African Identity of Biblical Persons and Nations, Volume 1 Teacher's guide (Black Light Fellowship, Second edition 1991)

Dr. John L. Johnson, The Black Biblical Heritage (Johnson Books Inc., 25 Edition. 2016)

Rev. Dr. F.S. Rhoades, Blacks in Every Book in the Bible – A study Guide (1995)

Lessie Myles, Discovering Black People in the Bible

Mawuli, The Bible is the Black Man's history Book (Nelson Research Services, London 2016)

James H. Warden JR, Blacks in the Bible – The Original Roots of Men and Women of Color in Scripture (Author House 2006)

Justice Randolph Jackson, Black People in the Bible (Original Roots Press, Second Edition 2013)

Rev. William Dwight McKissic SR., Beyond Roots: in Search of Blacks in the Bible (2017)

Richard Alburtus Morrisey, Bible History of the Negro (1915)

Onleiloue Chika Alston, Prophetic Whirlwind – Uncovering the Black Biblical Destiny (The Voices Publishing, 2nd edition 2022)

Dante Fortson, Pre-Slavery Christianity – It was never the White Man's religion (2019)

The Black Israelites

Gert Muller, The Ancient Black Hebrews – Abraham and his Family (Pomegranate Publishing, London 2021)

Gert Muller, The Ancient Black Hebrews Vol II – The Forensic Proof Simply explained (Pomegranate Publishing 2014)

Gert Muller, The Ancient Black Hebrews Vol III – The genetic Evidence (Pomegranate Publishing 2018)

Gert Muller, The Ancient Black Hebrews Vol IV – The Cover Up (Pomegranate Publishing 2018)

Ella J. Hughley, The Truth About Black Biblical Hebrews-Israelites (Jews) – The World's Best-Kept Secret (Hughley Publications, 9th printing 1982)

Jacqueline A French, The Great Awakening – Of the Black Hebrew Israelites…in these last days (G Publishing LLC 2017)

Anu M'Bantu and Gert Muller, The Ancient Black Hebrews and Arabs (Pomegranate Publishing 2013)

Arthur Koestler, The Thirteenth Tribe – The Khazar Empire and its Heritage (GSG & Associates Publishers 1976)

Sigmund Freud, Moses and Monotheism (Vintage Books 1939)

Dante Fortson, Undeniable – Full color evidence of Black Israelites in the Bible (2019)

Black Women in the Bible

Lessie Myles, Revealing (black) Women in the Bible

Dante Fortson, Lesser Known People of the Bible, Black Women

Dr. Theron D. Williams, Great Women of the Bible – Contemporary Conversations (The Bible in Black History Institute 2021)

Gert Muller, The Black Madonna, Christ, and the Black God and Goddess of the Bible (Pomegranate Publishing 2013)

Black Jesus

Evangelist T. C. Wanyanwu, Jesus is a Black Man (Amazon Kindle Direct Publishing, 2nd printing 2021)

William Mosley, What Color Was Jesus (5th edition 1987)

John G. Jackson, Was Jesus Christ a Negro? (African Tree Press)

Rabbi Simon Altaf Hakohen, Yahushua – The Black Messiah (Forever-Israel International Union of Qahalim 2nd Edition 2014)

www.ingramcontent.com/pod-product-compliance
Lightning Source LLC
Chambersburg PA
CBHW052030030426
42337CB00027B/4936